THE JOY OF STUDY

THE MACMILLAN COMPANY
NEW YORK · BOSTON · CHICAGO · DALLAS
ATLANTA · SAN FRANCISCO

MACMILLAN AND CO., LIMITED
LONDON · BOMBAY · CALCUTTA · MADRAS
MELBOURNE

THE MACMILLAN COMPANY
OF CANADA, LIMITED
TORONTO

The Joy of Study

Papers on New Testament

and Related Subjects

Presented to Honor

FREDERICK CLIFTON GRANT

———

EDITED BY *Sherman E. Johnson*

THE MACMILLAN COMPANY

New York: 1951

In 1930, while poking about in the public library of a small southern Illinois city, I came across a volume entitled *New Horizons of the Christian Faith*, by Frederick C. Grant. Having been brought up, like most Americans, to regard theology as a dry, antiquarian, and traditional exercise, I now learned for the first time what a world of intellectual vitality and vivid, relevant faith could be opened up to the inquirer. When, a few months later, I decided to study for the ministry, there was no doubt in my mind of the right place—the Western Theological Seminary, in Evanston, Illinois, of which Dr. Grant was then the dean.

One feature of the book that most impressed me was Dean Grant's enthusiasm for study—the sheer joy to be found by wallowing in the Old Testament, Tannaitic rabbinism, the New Testament, the Church Fathers, St. Thomas Aquinas, the Anglican divines. A middler in seminary sometimes found this overwhelming: how could one ever master the languages—not merely Latin, Greek and Hebrew, but the sesquipedalian technical words of German theology—and find one's way through a literature so vast? Yet this infectious joy of study was what helped the student to keep on trying, particularly since the teacher had come through his researches to a rich, firmly founded and loyal faith which he could preach with warmth and skill.

The tall, young, handsome dean of twenty-one years ago had already had a rich and varied ecclesiastical experience. Born in

Beloit, Wisconsin, in 1891, he spent his first years in that state, and after studying at Lawrence College came under the magical influence of two unusual biblical scholars—Fosbroke and Easton—at Nashotah House. Following his graduation at Nashotah, Mr. Grant went to the General Theological Seminary in New York, where a great director of graduate studies, Professor William H. P. Hatch, initiated him into textual criticism and introduced him to the works of a number of German New Testament scholars. After receiving his B.D. from General, he served churches in DeKalb and Dixon, Illinois, and continued his studies at the Western Theological Seminary in Chicago, where Easton was now professor. One of his earliest published articles, "The Permanent Value of the Primitive Christian Eschatology," which appeared in the *Biblical World* in 1917, showed the nature of his interests. Wrede, Schweitzer and Charles had put the whole world to studying eschatology. Grant, like everyone else, was in it, and he was also asking what it could mean to men of today.

From 1917 to 1920, Mr. Grant was assistant at St. Luke's Church, Evanston, and in full charge of that important parish while the rector, the late George Craig Stewart, was overseas as a chaplain. His next charge was Trinity Church, Chicago, of which he was rector from 1920 to 1924, and here he completed his work for the doctorate of theology at the Western Seminary. His dissertation was later expanded into the important monograph, *The Economic Background of the Gospels*, published by the Oxford University Press in 1926.

Two years were spent at Gambier, Ohio, as dean of Bexley Hall, and here some of Dr. Grant's vigor and talent as an administrator were disclosed. The year 1926–27 found him at the Berkeley Divinity School, then at Middletown, Connecticut, this time as professor of Systematic Theology. His theological interest, always lively, was deepened by the special studies then undertaken.

Dr. Grant was only thirty-six when the late Bishop Charles

Palmerston Anderson persuaded him to reorganize the Western Theological Seminary and move it to Evanston. Suitable candidates for the ministry were all too few in those days, and funds are always hard to come by, but Dr. Grant raised money, superintended construction of the magnificent Gothic buildings, gathered a competent faculty, allayed the fears of Evanston neighbors who did not want an "institution" next door, acted as father and pastor to the students, agonized over the budget, and saw to it that lights not needed were turned off in the dormitories. From 1927 to 1938 he presided over the seminary and was largely responsible for its merger (in 1933) with the Seabury Divinity School of Faribault, Minnesota, a stroke which saved both institutions in the dreadful days of the depression.

Despite the pressure of administrative detail, the joy of study was with him, and articles and books flowed from his pen. In 1938 he was called to the Edward Robinson chair of Biblical Theology at Union Theological Seminary, and now he was set relatively free to satisfy his great love for research and teaching. But Union has also made use of his administrative gifts, and for some years he has been deeply involved in the program of graduate studies both at Union and also at Columbia University, where his work is in the fields of Hellenistic and Roman religion. He is chairman of the Council on Graduate Studies in Religion, representing fifteen American and Canadian universities which confer the Ph.D. in Religion.

Dr. Grant's abounding health and energy, which we pray will be with him for many years to come, combined with his great industry and accuracy, have made it possible for him to cover wide fields with unusual thoroughness.

He has always been a churchman, a lover of his own communion and its activities. Many Sundays of each year have seen him in the pulpit or at the altar. On four occasions he has served as a deputy to the General Convention, he has been a member of the Joint Commission on Revision of the Hymnal and the Joint Commission on Approaches to Unity, and has written special studies for the Marriage Commission.

The same practical interest led him to write some of his earliest books for the use of Sunday school teachers and pupils. One of his first publications was a series of devotional addresses. For many years he worked at a book on *The Practice of Religion*, which finally appeared in 1946. *Christ's Victory and Ours* (1950) shows the same desire to relate New Testament and theology to people's everyday needs.

Loyal to his own denomination, he loves equally the Universal Church. His interest in reunion was manifest in his theological books, *New Horizons of the Christian Faith* and *Frontiers of Christian Thinking*. As a professor at Union Seminary, he has been in close touch with men of many churches. His work with the American Association of Theological Schools was an evidence of his talent for coöperation and his interest in the educational standards and administrative efficiency of seminaries all over the North American continent. He has many friends among the theological scholars of Great Britain and Europe, and some of them have been his students.

The Church has drawn heavily on his editorial skill. Since 1924 he has been editor of the *Anglican Theological Review*. For five years he was chairman of the editorial board of *The Witness*, and still serves as its book editor. He has edited two symposium volumes and participated in several others. Publishers know that he will meet deadlines.

It is difficult to get competent men to translate foreign theological works and still more difficult to secure publication. Dr. Grant made Bultmann and Kundsin for the first time available to many students by his translation, *Form Criticism* (1934). With three of his friends he published Johannes Weiss' *History of Primitive Christianity* in 1937. His version of Dibelius' *The Message of Jesus*

Christ (1939) is something of a *tour de force*. The Heidelberg scholar's racy German translation of the sayings is put into idiomatic English.

In many other ways Dr. Grant has fostered biblical research and teaching. He has been active in the work of the Society of Biblical Literature and is a former president of that body. He is a member of the revision committee which has produced the Revised Standard Version of the New Testament and which is now at work on the Old Testament. His article on "The Greek Text of the New Testament" in the *Introduction to the R. S. V.* packs a remarkable amount of wisdom into a short compass. He is also a member of the Versions Committee of the American Bible Society.

As a New Testament scholar, Dr. Grant is difficult to characterize. He does not belong to any one school or party. After 1914 the writings of Wrede and Schweitzer burst like a bombshell on English and American scholarship; he learned from the eschatological movement but was not carried away. Such also was his relation to the two Chicago movements—that of Burton and Goodspeed and the "social approach" represented by Shirley Jackson Case. He was greatly influenced by Streeter, but painstakingly worked over for himself the field covered by the members of Sanday's seminar. He has accepted the basic methods of form criticism but has worked out the details in his own way. An enthusiastic young man, writing in German and annoyed because *The Growth of the Gospels* (1933) did not go all the way with Dibelius and Bultmann, tried to explain Grant's preference for the Gospel of Luke as due to "the well-known aestheticism of the Episcopalian Church to which Professor Grant belongs." A better explanation would be Grant's knowledge of the Jewish background of Christianity and his historical tact.

His most constant preoccupation has been with the Synoptic Gospels and the life of Jesus. This has led him to a close examination of the Jewish background—not only in rabbinic and inter-testamental literature but in the Old Testament, of which he was professor in the Western Seminary. In more recent years his attention has turned to Hellenistic and Roman religion, which have such profound lessons to teach the student of Christian beginnings. Other phases of New Testament study have not been neglected. The chapter on the Fourth Gospel in *The Growth of the Gospels* was a pioneer work in English, and President Colwell of Chicago used to urge it on all his students. *An Introduction to New Testament Thought* (1950) shows other aspects of Dr. Grant's work—not least a sympathetic penetration into the ideas of St. Paul. Now as always he is fascinated by the Gospel of Mark. *The Earliest Gospel* (1943) is to be followed by a commentary on that book in *The Interpreter's Bible*, now in press.

Dr. Grant's insistence on seeing all sides of a problem has led him away from quick generalizations. Students have often found him—particularly in his earlier books—hard to read and get hold of because he would not say a clear Yes or No when the sources permit no such answer. His publications are full of instruction for those who will share his joy of study and follow him in his reasoning. One may venture the opinion that, because of his synoptic view and his painstaking accuracy, his works will be studied by New Testament scholars for a long time to come.

His work has been crowned by the honors that naturally attend such a distinguished career, and in these his students and colleagues take delight. They join in dedicating these essays to him in honor of his sixtieth birthday, and their wish is εἰς πολλὰ ἔτη.

                               SHERMAN E. JOHNSON

Cambridge, Massachusetts
February 2, 1951

Contents

THE JOY OF STUDY

The Parable of the Guests at the Banquet: A Sketch of the History of Its Interpretation

by FRANCIS W. BEARE

Trinity College, Toronto

The Parable of the Guests at the Banquet is transmitted in two versions, one in the Gospel according to St. Matthew (22:1–14), the other in the Gospel according to St. Luke (14:15–24). It is generally agreed that the two Evangelists are presenting the same parable,[1] but that they have not drawn it from any common written source.[2] Since the time of Jülicher,[3] moreover, most commentators have been agreed in judging that even the simpler Lucan form has been modified and extended under the influence of allegorizing tendencies to the extent of introducing a meaning that did not belong to the story originally told by Jesus. The expansions of Matthew, of course, are far more extensive and obvious; the process of allegorization has been carried ever so much further; and it is probable that another parable of a quite different tenor

[1] Many of the older commentators held that these were two distinct parables, chiefly because they felt obliged to harmonize the gospels; Gregory the Great, however, is willing to admit that they are the same in origin, and to explain the differences.

[2] B. W. Bacon argues that the parable is taken from Q (*Studies in Matthew* [New York, 1930], pp. 65 ff.); and T. W. Manson takes the same view (*The Sayings of Jesus* [London, 1949], p. 129). If this is so, one of the Evangelists at least has gone to unusual pains to alter the wording of the source, for the two versions have very few words in common.

[3] *Die Gleichnisreden Jesu*, 2d ed., rev. (Tübingen, 1910), pp. 407–433.

has been conflated with it. In the enlarged Matthaean form, the
parable was submitted to an increasingly thorough allegorical
interpretation, so that the history of its exegesis offers an interesting illustration of the methods and principles of the Fathers
and of the influence of theology upon exegesis. But it is worth
noticing at the outset that the process of alchemy has made a
good start within the canonical scriptures themselves. Here, as
generally, the theories of the *sola scriptura* school are refuted by
the facts; there is no sound basis for making a radical separation
between Scripture and the history of Christian thought, or for
postulating a unity in the New Testament or in the Bible as a
whole, distinct from the unity of the Christian faith which the
Holy Scriptures share with the church of the centuries.

The secondary elements in the Lucan version are relatively
slight. The Evangelist has given the parable its setting: it forms
the fourth of a group of pericopes more or less artificially linked
together around the theme of "banquet." There is first a healing
at a banquet (Luke 14:1–6); then a saying about precedence in
the banqueting-hall (vv. 7–11); then a saying about inviting the
needy to banquets (vv. 12–14); and finally the parable, which is
introduced as the response of Jesus to the pious ejaculation of a
guest: "Blessed is he who shall eat bread in the kingdom of God,"
for which the way has been prepared by the reference to "the
resurrection of the just" (v. 14). The Evangelist is perhaps also
responsible for the framing of the words in which the invited
guests beg off at the last moment (vv. 18–20); but it is at least
equally possible that Matthew has compressed these graphic
touches into the concise report: "They made light of it and went
off, one to his farm, another to his business" (Matt. 22:5). Much
more significance attaches to Luke's doubling of the invitation
to the new guests (v. 23), and to the closing pronouncement: "I tell
you, none of those men who were invited shall taste my banquet"
(v. 24). These words make explicit Luke's intention to present

the parable as an allegory of the reprobation of Israel and the extension of the gospel to the Gentiles. The effect is the same whether we take them as part of the parable, spoken by the host, or as a comment upon it, addressed by Jesus to his auditors. The doubling of the slave's mission to summon other guests reflects Luke's conception (historically sound, of course) of the stages in the extension of the gospel—first to the disinherited of Israel, "the poor and maimed and blind and lame" (v. 21, taken from the saying of Jesus in v. 13); then to the world without (v. 23).

When these Lucan accretions are removed, it would appear that we have recovered substantially the original form of the parable, which might be outlined as follows. A wealthy man invited many guests to a banquet at his home. At the last moment they all begged off, on the pretense of more pressing engagements, and the host in anger sent his slave out into the streets to invite the beggars of the town in their place. It has been suggested that some such thing had recently occurred in the neighborhood, and that Jesus is making his own application of a bit of local news.[4]

It is still not clear in what way he meant to apply it. Commentators appear to be agreed that it is rightly taken as a rebuke to the religious leaders of Israel, the scribes and Pharisees: confident as they are in their high privilege, assured of places at the Messianic banquet, they are in fact rejecting the call which Jesus is even now extending to them, and the publicans and sinners are being brought into the kingdom in their place. There are, however, difficulties in the way of this interpretation, and one is tempted to feel that it is unduly influenced by the artificial setting in which the parable has been placed by the Evangelists. The excuses given by the unwilling guests—"I have bought a field. . . . I have bought five yoke of oxen. . . . I have married a wife" do not in the least suggest the kind of fault that is particularly characteristic of the

---

[4] B. T. D. Smith, *The Parables of the Synoptic Gospels* (Cambridge, 1937), p. 202.

scribes and Pharisees. It is probable, therefore, that we ought to look for a broader interpretation, and see in the parable a much more general warning against the danger of losing the heavenly by absorption in the ordinary concerns of this world. Again, it is difficult to suppose that Jesus would think particularly of the religious *leaders* of Israel as peculiarly "those who had been invited"; it is surely the whole people that has been taught to set its hopes on the Kingdom of God; and it is the people generally that is turning a deaf ear to the invitation to repent and believe the gospel.

In the Matthaean version, the accretions are much more extensive and the allegory has been given a different pointing. The householder of Luke's story has become a king, and the banquet a wedding-feast which he gives for his son. Thus on the familiar Jewish representation of the Kingdom of God under the figure of a great banquet has been superimposed the specifically Christian symbolism of Christ as the Bridegroom and the Messianic Banquet as the mystical marriage of Christ and the Church. The one slave has been multiplied into a numerous domestic establishment; [5] and the slaves are sent twice to summon the invited guests. At this point, Matthew introduces a quite incongruous addition. The invited guests are not content merely to plead more pressing business as an excuse for not coming to the banquet, but proceed to maltreat and even to kill the king's slaves; and the king sends his troops to destroy the murderers and to burn their city. Yet the rest of the story presupposes that the guests live in the same city as their host, and that others are being gathered to fill the ban-

---

[5] Some commentators think that the shoe is on the other foot—that it is Luke who has reduced the householder's slaves to one, that he may represent Christ as the bearer of God's invitation. J. M. Creed's rebuttal: "Luke does not allegorize" (*Gospel acc. to St. Luke* [London, 1930], *ad loc.*) is not a sufficient refutation, for there is an element of allegory in Luke's version. But the story does not really demand more than one slave for the service of the householder, whereas once the host is made into a king, the single slave would be an absurdity in the story.

queting-hall even while the armies are being mustered and the city destroyed. It has been suggested that this intrusion is a fragment of another parable—a Parable of the Rebellious Citizens [6]—but it is more likely that Matthew has simply transposed the theme of the preceding Parable of the Vineyard and introduced it here in this new form without regard for congruity, to develop the allegory of Israel's rejection of the gospel and its punishment. Following this, there is no place for an appeal to "the poor and maimed and blind and lame" from the streets and lanes of the city, since the whole nation has come under judgment and is reprobate; there remains only the great Gentile mission, figured under the "both bad and good" who are summoned from the thoroughfares (the highways outside?) to fill the king's house. After this comes a second incongruous addition, in this case almost certainly a fragment of another parable.[7] Although the story would imply that the new guests have been brought from the thoroughfares just as they were, the king finds fault with one who has no wedding garment and commands his attendants to bind him hand and foot and to cast him into the outer darkness. And although only one guest is thus cast out, Matthew concludes with the saying of Jesus, undoubtedly authentic, but out of place in this context: "For many are called, but few are chosen." Whatever the lesson of the parable, it is not this!

The setting of the parable is again the responsibility of the Evangelist. In its immediate context, it is paired with the Parable of the Vineyard (21:33–43), having in common with it the theme of the Jewish rejection of God's messengers, its punishment, and the transference of the divine blessing to the Gentiles. More widely, it forms part of a long series of pericopes of varied character which are linked by the common theme of the conflict

[6] T. W. Manson, *The Teaching of Jesus* (Cambridge, 1931), pp. 83 ff.
[7] Possibly a rabbinic parable, such as that told by R. Johanan ben Zacchai (*Shabb.* 153a; translated in Bacon, *op. cit.*, pp. 72 f.).

between Jesus and the religious leaders—chief priests, scribes,
elders, Pharisees, Sadducees (21:12–23:39); and all of this is intro-
ductory to the warnings of judgment which form the substance of
cc. 24 and 25. In Matthew's view, therefore, the overriding theme
of the parable is judgment—first the judgment of God upon rebellious Israel, and then the final judgment of all who profess to
follow Christ, according to their works. In his hands, the parable
has taken the shape of "a sketch of the history of salvation from
the appearance of the prophets through the destruction of Jerusalem to the Last Judgment." [8] For him, its central lesson is that
just as the Jews have been punished for their rejection of Jesus, so
the *corpus permixtum* ("both bad and good") of the great Gentile
church will be judged, and those who have not brought forth the
fruits of holiness will be cast into outer darkness.

In the hands of the two Evangelists, then, the parable has received a measure of allegorization. Each in his own way has reshaped his material and embellished it with new elements in order
to make still clearer the interpretation which he understands to be
in it. But in neither case has it been transformed into a full-blown
allegory. There are plainly many features which belong simply to
the furniture of the story, to which neither Evangelist attaches an
allegorical significance. For such an interpreter as Origen, however, the parable is constructed from beginning to end as an
allegory, and there can be no smallest detail without its own significance. As all later interpreters draw directly or indirectly upon
him, we may give his exposition in some fullness.

The human king means, tropically, the God and Father of
Christ Jesus; the marriage of the king's son is the restoration of
Christ's Church, the Bride, to Christ, her Bridegroom; the servants
sent to call those who had been invited to the marriage are the
prophets who sought by their predictions to turn the members of

[8] J. Jeremias, *Die Gleichnisse Jesu* (*Abhandlungen zur Theologie des
Alten und Neuen Testaments*, No. 11: Zürich, 1947), p. 44.

the People towards the joy which was to come at the restoration
of the Church to Christ; those who refused to come although they
had been invited in advance are those who did not hearken to the
words of the prophets; the other servants sent out are another band
of prophets; the banquet prepared, for which the king's bulls and
fatlings have been sacrificed, is the solid and spiritual food of the
mysteries of God. So also the "all things ready" are the discourses
concerning all ultimate realities (*hoi peri pantôn tôn ontôn logoi*)
whereof those who have responded to the call shall eat and drink,
when that which is perfect is come. Then is prophesied the war
against the Jews and the taking of Jerusalem, and the slaughter of
the People, after the sojourn of Christ.

The passage, "Then he says to his slaves . . . As many as you
find, invite to the banquet," may be compared to the Apostles of
Jesus Christ saying, "It was necessary that the Gospel be first pro-
claimed to you, but since you judge yourselves unworthy, lo, we
turn to the Gentiles." The thoroughfares are the realms outside
of Israel, wherein those found by the apostles were called to the
wedding.

On "both bad and good" he comments:

The Apostles did not care whether the called, before their calling, were bad or good; for they called all who were to be found.
. . . The outcome was not to be that the bad should remain bad,
but that they should change their habits, putting off such garments
as were unsuited to the wedding, and putting on such as were
proper to the wedding, viz., "bowels of mercies, kindness, humility,
gentleness, longsuffering." . . . These are the wedding-garments.[9]

It might seem that Origen had fully expounded the significance
of the allegory, but in his own view he has made no more than a
good start. "Let this be taken as a rough general account of the
parable," he says, "but we shall return now and try to explore it
in accordance with its inherent force, if perchance with the aid of
the Holy Spirit we may be able to find and build some deeper

[9] *Comm. in Matt.*, xvii, pp. 791–803.

thoughts upon the parable, and according to what is fitting, to be
silent, to speak in riddles, or to expound." [10] And so he discusses
the particular significance of the word "man" (*anthrôpos*) which
Matthew attaches to "king" with apparent redundance, and finds
in it a weapon to use against those who reject the Old Testament
because of its anthropomorphisms and anthropopathisms; he ex-
amines the different classes of those who appear in this similitude—
the king, his son, and especially the different types of subjects in
the kingdom, from which he deduces that there are many different
classes of souls which are known to God and are assigned according to their capacities either to be incorporated into the Bride or
to serve God in other modes. And he finds particular meanings in
the binding of the hands and feet of the reprobate and in the outer
darkness into which he is cast. In the burning of the city, too, he
finds that the meaning is not exhausted in the prophecy of the
destruction of Jerusalem by the Romans, but that it has a spiritual
sense. The king's armies, in this higher interpretation, are the heavenly hosts, or the avenging angels; the city of murderers is the
system of false doctrine framed in the wisdom of the rulers of this
world. And the oxen and fatlings of the feast represent respec-
tively the solid food of the gospel and the spiritual sweetnesses of
contemplation.

Irenaeus, deeply involved as he is in the conflict with Gnosti-
cism, employs the parable chiefly as an argument for the unity of
the God of the Old Testament with the God of the New, the
Just God with the Good God. The Lord who calls Christians by
the Apostles is the same as He who called the men of old by the
prophets; the divine King who invites men to enjoy the blessings
of the Marriage-feast is the same as He who condemns the despiser
to be cast into outer darkness.[11]

Later Greek commentators lay emphasis chiefly on the necessity of the wedding-garment. They agree that it signifies good

[10] *Ibid.*   [11] *Contra Haer.*, xxxvi, lviii.

works and an upright life; occasionally it is interpreted to mean the Holy Spirit. Chrysostom starts with the common interpretation: "The garment is life and conduct (*bios kai praxis*)," but proceeds with his customary zeal to apply it particularly to the monastic profession. "Remember those holy men of whom I discoursed to you yesterday, those who wear the garments of hair, who dwell in the deserts. These especially are those who wear the wedding-garments."[12]

Among the Latin Fathers, there is no general treatment of the parable before Jerome, whose brief annotations are clear and sober, according to his wont.[13] Augustine has two sermons on the passages, the one on the Matthaean version, the other on the Lucan; he regards them as different parables. The sermon on the passage in Matthew is directed against the Donatists, and is chiefly devoted to the exposition of the wedding-garment as denoting "love out of a pure heart and a good conscience and faith unfeigned." Such love will not despise the communion of the catholic church, as the Donatists are doing. "For the wedding-garment is received in honour of the Bridal, that is, of the Bridegroom and the Bride. You know the Bridegroom: it is Christ. You know the Bride: it is the Church."[14] In the sermon on the Lucan text, he offers a complete allegorical interpretation, with particular attention to the three excuses offered by the unwilling guests. The field that has been bought is insolent lordship; the five yoke of oxen are the solicitations of the five senses—these are called oxen, "because by those senses of the flesh earthly things are pursued, and oxen turn over the earth"; the wife is the delight of the flesh.[15] Then there is his fatal use of the text "compel them to come in" to justify the persecution of the Donatists.[16]

The increasing extravagance of allegorical interpretation, and

[12] *Hom. in Matt.*, lxix.   [13] *Comm. in Evang. Matt., ad loc.*
[14] Sermon 90.   [15] Sermon 112.
[16] Epistle 185, c. VI, sec. 23.

incidentally the increasing importance given to the Virgin, are seen in the exposition of Gregory the Great. In general, he follows the lines struck out by Origen and especially by Augustine, but he interprets the making of the Marriage primarily of the Incarnation.

> God the Father then made the marriage for his Son, when he united him to human nature in the womb of the Virgin. But since that union (of marriage) is as a rule made between two persons, be it far from our minds to believe that the Person of our Redeemer, God and Man, Jesus Christ, is formed by the union of two persons. It may therefore be said more openly and more safely that the Father made the marriage for the King, his Son, when he joined Holy Church to him through the mystery of the Incarnation. Now the womb of the Virgin was the chamber of the Bridegroom; wherefore the Psalmist says, "He hath set his tabernacle in the sun, and he himself is as a bridegroom proceeding out of his chamber." Thus it was as a bridegroom proceeds out of his chamber that the incarnate God proceeded out of the womb of the Virgin to unite the Church to himself.

In the interpretation of the wedding-garment, he follows Augustine in interpreting it as love. It cannot mean either baptism or faith, for the kingdom of God in the parable means the present church (*praesens ecclesia*), and no one enters it without baptism and faith. "What then are we to understand by the weddinggarment, if not charity?" [17]

Through the Middle Ages, there was little attempt at independent exposition; the teachers of the Church were content to form collections of extracts from the great expositors of the past. With the Reformation, however, there is a renaissance of biblical preaching and of scholarly exegesis; and again the particular theological emphasis of the time makes itself felt.

Luther wrote no commentary upon the Gospels. His interpretations are chiefly to be sought in the sermons which he preached

[17] *Hom. in Evang.*, 38.

on the different lections as they came to be read in the course of
the Christian year. The parable in the Gospel according to St. Matthew is read on the Twentieth Sunday after Trinity, and at least
three of Luther's sermons on it have been preserved. He assumes
that parables are allegories and that the true meaning does not lie
upon the surface. "This Gospel," he remarks, "presents to us the
parable of the wedding; therefore we are compelled to understand
it differently than it sounds and appears to the natural ear and eye.
Hence we will give attention to the spiritual meaning of the
parable and then notice how the text has been torn and perverted."
His own characteristic emphasis on justification by faith alone
comes out most clearly in the exposition of the significance of the
wedding-garment.

> Then the King will find one, not only a single person, but a
> large company, not clothed with a wedding garment, that is, with
> faith. These are pious people, . . . for you must consider them
> the ones who have heard and understood the Gospel, yet they
> cleaved to certain works and did not creep entirely into Christ;
> like the foolish virgins who had no oil, that is, no faith. To them
> the King will say: "Bind him hand and foot, and cast him into the
> outer darkness." That is, he condemns their good works, that they
> no longer avail anything; for the hands signify their work, the feet
> their walk in life; and he will then cast them into the outer dark-
> ness. . . . Now the wedding garment is Christ himself, which is
> put on by faith, as the Apostle says in Rom. 13:14: "Put ye on the
> Lord Jesus Christ." Then the garment gives forth a lustre of itself,
> that is, faith in Christ bears fruit of itself, namely, love which
> works through faith in Christ.

And in another sermon he remarks in like vein:

> This wedding garment must be the new light of the heart,
> kindled in the heart by the knowledge of the graciousness of this
> bridegroom and his wedding feast. Then the heart will wholly
> cleave to Christ, and, transfused by such comfort and joy, will so

live and do as it knows to be pleasing unto him, even as a bride
towards the bridegroom. This St. Paul calls "putting on the Lord
Christ" . . . which takes place especially through faith, by which
the heart is renewed and purified, and of which thereupon also the
fruits—provided it be true faith—follow and prove themselves. On
the other hand, where there is no faith, there also the Holy Ghost
is not, nor such fruits as please God.[18]

Melanchthon gives concise expression to the same fundamental
doctrine:

He shows the difference between true believers and the hypocrites, who in outward show are in the Church and at the banquet, and none the less do not truly believe, do not adore the
Bridegroom, have not, he says, a wedding garment. I withhold any
long and manifold discussions about the garment, and say simply:
the wedding garment is true and living faith, which is experienced
in true penitence, and lifts up the heart, and kindles true prayer,
hope and confession, and the other fruits which ought to follow
thereupon. This faith, true and unfeigned, is the wedding garment,
as it is said in Hosea: "I will betroth thee to me in faith." [19]

Calvin in general renounces the allegorical method and seeks
as far as possible to give the plain sense of the words of Scripture.
Evidently the interpretation of the wedding-garment had become
a vexed question in the controversy over the doctrines of the Re-
formers; for he begins his discussion of this part of the parable
with the words: "As to the wedding-garment, is it faith, or is it a
holy life?" And he gives the sober answer: "This is a useless controversy, for faith cannot be separated from good works, nor do
good works proceed from any other source than from faith." And
he concludes: "The words of Christ mean nothing more than this,
that the external profession of faith is not a sufficient proof that

---

[18] *Luther's Church Postil: Gospels*, Vol. V, tr. J. N. Lenker (Minneapolis,
1905), pp. 227, 230, 234, 250–51.
[19] *Brev. Comm. in Matt., ad loc.*

God will acknowledge as his people all who appear to have taken their place in the ranks beneath his banner." [20]

On the saying, "Compel them to come in," he comments that "this is a display of the astonishing goodness of God, who . . . not only arouses us by exhortations, but as it were compels us by threatenings, to draw near to him." This already goes beyond the proper sense of the words—"the idea of literal compulsion is not at all suggested" (Creed); certainly the slave is not expected to threaten them with dire penalties if they refuse the invitation; Calvin, in spite of his exegetical principles, is here allowing himself to be affected by the allegorical tradition. Unfortunately, he goes still further, and commends Augustine's use of the words to justify compulsion in the matter of religion. "I do not disapprove of the use which Augustine frequently made of this passage against the Donatists, to prove that godly princes may lawfully issue edicts for compelling obstinate and rebellious persons to worship the true God, and to maintain the unity of the faith; for though faith is voluntary, yet we see that such methods are useful for subduing the obstinacy of those who will not yield unless they are thus compelled." [21] Truly a strange wresting of the Word of God to serve his own purposes, on the part of the great Reformer! And a strange argument from expediency.

Calvin marks a great advance over all previous commentators in the critical perception that the order in which the Gospel writers arrange their materials is often determined by themselves, not fixed by tradition. Thus he has no difficulty in recognizing that he has indeed before him two versions of the one parable, though they differ both in the setting and in numerous details. He

[20] *Commentary on a Harmony of the Evangelists*, Vol. II, tr. W. Pringle (Edinburgh, 1845), *ad loc*. Nowhere do I find any justification for Lagrange's statement that the wedding-garment "according to the early Protestants, means the Lutheran faith, that which justifies without works" (*L'Évangile selon Saint Matthieu* [Paris, 1927], *ad loc*.).

[21] *Ibid.*

sees that Matthew has grouped this with other materials which bear upon the controversy of Jesus with the religious leaders. "The design which Matthew had in view was to point out the reasons why the scribes were excited to the highest pitch of fury; and therefore he properly placed it in the midst of those discourses which were hateful to them, and interwove it with those discourses, without attending to the order of time." Likewise, he perceives that the differences largely reflect the characteristic methods of the evangelists. "Matthew and Luke differ in this respect, that Matthew details many circumstances, while Luke states the matter summarily, and in a general manner. . . . But we have formerly pointed out a similar distinction, that Matthew, in explaining the same thing, is more copious, and enters into fuller details. There is a remarkable agreement between them in the main points of the parable." [22]

The interpretation of this parable, as of all the parables, enters upon a new phase in modern times with the epoch-making work of Jülicher. He insisted that the parable is "not an allegory requiring to be skilfully deciphered, but a story that anyone could understand." [23] And the latest advance of all is made by the relatively new science of Form Criticism, with the realization that the tradition has been continuously reshaped in its transmission by the experience of the living church and the needs of its teaching; that "the early Church explains and amplifies the parable of Jesus in accordance with its own concrete situation." [24]

[22] *Ibid.*
[23] *Op. cit.* (n. 3), p. 432.
[24] Jeremias, *op. cit.*, p. 27.

The Teachings of Jesus and Pacifism

by BURTON H. THROCKMORTON, JR.
Union Theological Seminary

Once again Christians in most of the world are faced with the problem of the response they should make to the summons of their various governments to take active part in war. It is the purpose of this paper to investigate the relationship of Jesus' teachings to participation in war and to shed some light, if possible, on the practical decision which Christians must make.

I should like to say at the outset that I do not believe proof-texts can ever solve the problem, for the following reasons:

(1) The gospels record no saying of our Lord either commanding or forbidding participation of his followers in war.

(2) If proof-texts be cited as being indirectly related to active participation in war, they may be cited on the sides of both resistance and non-resistance. Jesus said, "Do not resist one who is evil." [1] He also said, "Render to Caesar the things that are Caesar's" [2] and "Do not think that I have come to bring peace on earth; I have not come to bring peace, but a sword." [3] If Jesus' example be cited as authoritative, one can point to his own resistance as well as non-resistance to evil. Moreover, proof-texts employed

[1] Matt. 5:39.　　　　[2] Matt. 22:21.　　　　[3] Matt. 10:34.
(All New Testament quotations are taken from the Revised Standard Version, Thomas Nelson & Sons, New York, 1946.)

in support of a particular ethical act are too often summoned to substantiate a pre-conceived conclusion; the action does not result from the text, but the text is used to validate the act. This is especially true when proof-texts can be cited on both sides of the issue involved. One who bases his argument on a proof-text can seldom be argued out of his position no matter how many texts supporting the contrary view are put before him. Even if the manuscript support for his text is shown to be extremely weak, he will claim it not because his challenger's logic with regard to the text is unconvincing, but because bias with regard to his own opinion is unyielding. So I shall not cite proof-texts substantiating or repudiating participation in war; they are all listed in books for or against pacifism.

(3) Any saying of Jesus which might possibly be construed indirectly to relate to the taking up of arms, or the refusal of doing so, ought not necessarily to be applied to modern techniques of war about which Jesus knew nothing, or to the total world scene as it appears today. Modern warfare is so different quantitatively from ancient warfare as to have become different qualitatively. A sanction by Jesus of what to us would be a very minor skirmish ought not too easily to be said to imply a similar sanction of atomic bomb attacks. The two situations are not sufficiently analogous. Similarly, a forbidding by Jesus of a Jewish revolt against Rome, should such be discovered, would not necessarily imply that Jesus would likewise disapprove of a United Nations force maintaining a semblance of peace somewhere in the world.

To what, then, in the gospels shall we appeal in our attempt to throw light on this question? I believe we must appeal to the basic command of Jesus: "You shall love the Lord your God with all your heart, and with all your soul, and with all your mind," and "you shall love your neighbor as yourself. On these two commandments depend all the law and the prophets." [4] Everything was

---

[4] Matt. 22:37, 39–40.

judged by Jesus to be right or wrong according as it fulfilled or did not fulfill this command. No action contradicting this command, no matter what other ethical saying it might fulfill, can be defended as praiseworthy to God as revealed in Christ.

But, unfortunately, in many instances a Christian must make a choice between two lines of action, neither one of which fulfills this command. This fact is not always recognized. Professor G. H. C. Macgregor writes, "It is impossible to believe that God will ever face the wholly consecrated Christian with a dilemma in which there is only a choice of two evils." [5] Likewise, Leyton Richards: "No Christian need be caught in such a dilemma; for there is always an exit from a choice of evils by the way of the Cross or its equivalent, if only men have sufficient faith to take it." [6] I agree wholeheartedly that when martyrdom presents itself to a Christian as an alternative to a choice between evils, it is the path he must take as a follower of his Blessed Lord. This fact lies at the very heart of the gospel message. But I cannot agree that such a path is always a live option. There are times when no ideal possibility of action presents itself, and it is quite wrong to identify non-resistance with martyrdom. On many occasions non-resistance is much further removed from martyrdom than is resistance. If a gangster holds up my wife, beats her, takes what she has, and makes off with it, my non-resistance would have nothing to do with martyrdom; but my resistance of the gangster on my wife's behalf might well lead to death, if not martyrdom. Martyrdom is not always a possibility, and the Christian is sometimes presented with the dilemma of a choice between evils.

Not only is martyrdom, negatively speaking, not always a possibility—although it is such when one is himself under attack—but there are also occasions when non-resistance is neither an ideal

---

[5] G. H. C. Macgregor, *The New Testament Basis of Pacifism*, London, 1937, p. 145.

[6] Quoted by Macgregor, *op. cit.*, p. 145.

solution nor preferable to resistance. It is sometimes stated by theologians defending the non-resistance point of view that they never sanction any ways of meeting evil which are not redemptive, and that non-resisting love leads to redemption. I quote again from Dr. Macgregor: "The Christian will never freely and personally participate in any methods of meeting evil which he does not believe to be ultimately redemptive." [7] But how can *any* man— Christian or non-Christian—in our society avoid participating in methods of meeting evil which are not redemptive? (Of course, if one says *ultimately redemptive*, one can allow for any kind of activity, for one could conceivably believe any act to be *ultimately* redemptive as all ultimate issues are in the hands of God. It is the non-pacifist who should use the word in this connection. But let us understand the quotation in the sense in which it is relevant from the pacifist point of view.) I cannot believe that terms served in prison are often redemptive; yet most pacifists agree that the application of force on some level is necessary. They will co-operate with the police and courts of law. Dr. Macgregor himself, in order to justify his own personal sanction of a police force, says that Jesus' "way will permit the use of force"—though he adds, "only within the strictest limits." [8] Even he, a staunch pacifist, acknowledges the necessity for the use of force and then declares that such force is compatible with Jesus' own (pacifist) way of life. But once a pacifist acknowledges the necessity for the use of force and then sanctions his belief that force is necessary by an appeal to the gospel, his argument for non-resistance as a principle breaks down. Force and non-resistance are opposite concepts and self-contradictory. If non-resistance is *always* right, as a principle, then force is *never* right. Does Dr. Macgregor believe that force applied against one person is redemptive, whereas force applied against a group of people is not?

Secondly, there are occasions when non-resisting love is *not*

[7] *Ibid.*, p. 146.   [8] *Ibid.*, p. 51.

redemptive (i.e., in any immediate sense where it can be observed —in the only sense in which any human action can ever be said to be redeeming; all final salvation is of God, only) and is irrelevant unless it takes the form of loyalty to justice or of resisting love. Dr. Macgregor writes, "Sacrificial love redeems and changes the evil will." [9] But does it always? My non-resisting love for the gangster while he beats my wife is "sacrificial" only in the sense that I sacrifice my wife to a criminal who beats her, not, presumably, because it is God's will but, more probably, because it is the criminal's will; and such non-resistance will undoubtedly not change his intentions or alter the outcome of the event. At the time, it will probably be an irrelevant factor. Non-resistance would not be redemptive for the criminal, though its motive might well be love. At the moment of the event, redemption is not an issue primarily involved, though it may become an issue after the event when, if caught, the man may respond to forgiveness. The pacifist too quickly identifies redemption with non-resisting love. Non-resistance in the case of an attack upon one's self might well reveal love which could redeem; but one's non-resistance in the case of attack on someone else contains, it would seem, a very small redemptive possibility. And I find no word in the gospels which commands this.

Furthermore, there are occasions when love must take the form of loyalty to justice, or must be expressed to one at the expense of another, when the more ideal solution which love would prefer is impossible to realize. It is in the former case and, perhaps, to an extent in the latter also, that the concept of justice must be related to Christ's command to love. If a nation supplies food to another nation which is hungry, or goes to its aid when it is being attacked, its motive could be either compassion and affection, or the establishment of justice, or some combination of the two; but in any event, the root of the motive would be the same—love, in varying

[9] *Ibid.*, p. 95.

degrees. (Of course, if the motive were purely selfish, the action could have no gospel justification.) P. T. Forsyth wrote, "Righteousness is the form divine love takes between men in nations." [10] Though one might not agree that righteousness is the only form divine love can take between men in nations, one would certainly agree that righteousness, or the establishment of justice, is often a form taken by love. Or, to put it another way, one ought not consider the establishment of justice and the manifestation of love as though they were unrelated.

The pacifist position, it seems to me, too often ignores the whole concept of justice, or righteousness, as soon as it becomes necessary to defend the just by force. It will defend the just in the realm of argument and debate, but as soon as the unjust side uses force to accomplish its end, the pacifist will appeal not to justice, but to love—affection—when the establishment of justice is the immediate issue, if not the ultimate one. Love is not necessarily less present when force becomes involved in the establishment of justice. One enhances justice because one loves; indeed one may defend the just out of a love which offers its life.

The just side is too often abandoned to fare for itself as soon as it is attacked by violent means. Admittedly, defense of one side means attack on its opposite; but if one takes no action at all, he fails in his obligation to the just. To be sure, in such a situation, no possible action completely fulfills the law of Christ; one must choose the less evil of two evil ways.

Love also must often be expressed to one at the expense of another. Love does not prefer so to express itself; but there are times when not to express itself in such a way is not to express itself at all. To take our previous example once more: Is one who has been commanded to love, to stand by and watch a gangster beat his wife? Or, should love for one's wife impel one to defend her? It would appear that non-resistance in such a circumstance

[10] P. T. Forsyth, *The Christian Ethic of War*, London, 1916, p. 104.

would imply some denial of a professed love, for it is an inherent
attribute of love to defend whom and what it loves. The Hebrews
knew of a certainty that God loved them because they were delivered from the hands of their enemies; and God's love both for
Christ and for man in Christ would never have been revealed had
not God rescued Christ from the power of sin and death in the
resurrection. The love revealed in the resurrection involved injury
on the Cross. The love of God is revealed in the Cross precisely
because the pain which the Son endured there was inflicted by the
Father. "Love in God so dealt with the whole moral situation of
the race, its holy righteousness so dealt with a grand world-
unrighteousness, as to inflict the violence of the Cross, sparing not
even His Son. . . . God so loved, on such a principle, so un-
sparingly, as to do that Son's body and soul the 'injury' of the
Cross." [11]

We come finally to the issue of military service. How shall one
relate the commandment of Christ to his response to his government's call to active duty? We have tried to show that the Christian frequently faces a dilemma of a choice between evils in which
martyrdom is not a possibility; that the use of force and coöperation with force is incumbent upon all men, living as they do in a
world not yet freed from the power of sin; that human love
cannot always act redemptively and should not stultify action;
and finally that the defense of justice does not preclude love, and
while defense of the just, expressed in action, temporarily involves
resistance to the unjust, such conduct is more compatible with
love than is inactivity.

Anyone who will agree that on some level the application of
force is necessary for a right cause cannot logically state that the
use of force in warfare is wrong in principle. He may only say
that it becomes wrong because too much force is involved. It is at
this point that the pacifist leaves his defense of justice and flees to

[11] *Ibid.*, p. 45.

his argument on behalf of love, declaring that on this larger scale
of international relations love becomes redemptive, whereas on the
smaller scale of the thief and the pickpocket justice must be defended by force. Here, it seems to me, is an indefensible incon-
sistency. Moreover, the defense of justice does not at all imply that
love is being forsaken. To take up arms is not to abandon Christ's
command, although it is not, on the other hand, to fulfill it completely.

But this is not to say that every time a war is declared the duty
of a Christian is to take up arms. This is the position taken by the
strict militarist who conceives it his duty to fight at the moment
his government becomes involved in war. One sometimes hears a
Christian defend his participation in war by saying that Jesus'
ethical teachings are not workable in modern society, and that
even the principles lying behind the teachings are too lofty to be
relevant to ordinary daily life. I agree that the principles are lofty,
but I do not agree that they are not to be applied. The Church
must now, as it did in the first centuries of its history, take Jesus'
teachings seriously and hold them up as the criteria by which her
members must act. It is the duty of the Church to apply the teachings now in a society quite different from that in which they were
first given. Jesus intended his teachings to be directly relevant to
the lives of his hearers in the situation in which they then found
themselves, i.e., in *this* world as it existed then and as it exists
today. Therefore his teachings are immediately applicable to the
lives of his followers of all generations, and their primary purpose
is not to condemn but to guide. They presuppose evil, and were
therefore intended not for the Kingdom of God, completely realized, but for this world still under the power of sin, but into which
the Kingdom has broken.[12]

---

[12] For an excellent discussion of the nature of Jesus' ethical teachings, and
for the point of view regarding them assumed in this paper, see Frederick C.
Grant's *An Introduction to New Testament Thought*, New York, 1950, ch. XII.

A Christian's duty is not first to his government and then to God; and before a Christian can participate in war (or, for that matter, in any use of force) he must ask himself two questions:

First, Is there here a case of injustice? Very often, of course, this cannot be known with any certainty; there is some justification for both sides of the controversy. But the question must be asked and an answer sought, and no Christian ought to take up arms to defend what he believes to be an unjust cause. Not, "Our country, right or wrong"; [13] but, Our country only if she is right. Defense of an injustice can never be sanctioned on the basis of the gospel, but defense of justice can. Justice is a characteristic of God in both the Old and New Testaments, and the establishment of justice a virtue in both.

My love for Stalin or for Russian communists would be irrelevant in the event of war; and if the Russian army were suddenly to flood the whole of Europe and Russian bombers were to head for American shores, the only relevant action I could take would be one based on a consideration of the justice or injustice involved. If I decided that the injustice far exceeded the justice, I would have to use the most effective means for dealing with an injustice carried out by force.

But there is a second question the Christian must ask: Can I participate in the means which my state has adopted to deal with this circumstance? And here the problem in modern times becomes most acute. A Christian might decide that his duty lies in protecting those who have been wronged and his motive might be love. (If it is other than love, his action would have no gospel justification.) But so to decide is not automatically to approve any measure taken by his government, which acts, of necessity, on the level of justice and not on the level of pure love. The penalty which is enforced must be in relation to the crime. If, in the case of a local police force, the penalty is unjust, it is the law that must

[13] Stephen Decatur, *Toast Given at Norfolk*, April, 1816.

be changed, and not the police force discarded. But as yet there is nothing which could be regarded as law to deal with international warfare, and there is no international army which could enforce such a law. As a result, national armies may use any means of destruction at their disposal, the curbing feature being not law, but primarily fear of retaliation. So a Christian entering the armed services in effect subscribes to participation in any form of warfare which his superiors command. It is as though he were subscribing to a police force which could either jail, hang, poison, or burn a thief—the penalty being possibly far in excess of the crime.

This situation presents a problem which grows increasingly serious, for the weapons of modern warfare are potentially far more destructive than any cause, no matter how just, could warrant the use of. Though a Christian may agree that it would be unjust for a massive Russian army and uncounted Russian planes to flood in and over the whole of Europe, terrorizing and despotically ruling two whole continents against the wills of millions of men; and though he may agree that it is his duty to defend his family and friends and what he believes to be a superior way of life from a like atrocity at home, and to aid in throwing off the tyrannical yoke from the necks of his fellow men abroad; he has still to ask himself whether he can associate himself actively with the possible means whereby this will be attempted. In short, he must ask such a question as this: Could I obey the order to command a force which would annihilate the city of Paris and all her inhabitants, should I be so instructed? Could the end in view justify this means? Possibly yes, possibly no. Who can tell another? I think no one. This is a question which must be decided, but which can only be decided by a man on his knees before God. No one has a right to tell another, for no one knows with absolute assurance.

Jesus' command is to love—God and one's fellow men—and if need be to lay down one's life for his brothers; but justice must be enforced in the world in which we have been set. On occasion it is directly relevant where pure love is only indirectly so, or not immediately relevant at all. And it is on such occasions that the Christian's duty lies in defending the just against the unjust, which action does not deny love, but may affirm it. Whether a case of injustice is actually involved is sometimes difficult or even impossible to determine. But a decision must be sought by the best light available, for to make no decision and to remain inactive is also to influence the outcome.

Having made this decision, one must make a second, also difficult: he must ask, Is the more just side using just means to establish justice? Or are the means more evil than the injustice being resisted? No one can finally decide either question for anyone else, especially the latter. The final question must always be, What word has God spoken to me? The pacifist is in error when he insists that on the basis of Jesus' teachings resistance is *always* wrong; and the non-pacifist is in error when he insists that resistance is always the clear duty implicit under attack—the call may be rather to martyrdom or to a rejection of the defense of an injustice. Both the pacifist and non-pacifist positions reflect a legalism—the assumption that the performance or non-performance of a particular act is always right, under all circumstances. There is only one law in the gospel—the law of love—and no other law is always binding. Each circumstance requires its own response to be made in accordance with the light which God has given to those who seek his face in Jesus Christ, our Lord.

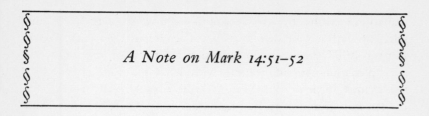

A Note on Mark 14:51–52

by JOHN KNOX
Union Theological Seminary

One of the most perplexing passages in the Gospels is the story in Mark 14:51–52 of the young man clad only in a linen cloth (σινδών) who was seized at the moment of Jesus' arrest, but escaped leaving the linen cloth in the hands of his captors. The presence of this pericope has always created a problem, not only because of the apparent insignificance of the incident it records, but also because it interrupts an otherwise restrained and moving account of the final tragic episode in Jesus' career, the story of the Passion itself. Anyone who has read this Markan narrative (chs. 14–15) to a congregation on Good Friday is bound to have felt tempted to omit this apparently whimsical passage. Not only is there no break whatever in the continuity of the narrative when these verses are left out, but the dramatic effectiveness of the somber story is greatly enhanced. It is not surprising that both Matthew and Luke pass over it.

So far as I know, three explanations of the strange appearance of this pericope have been offered—all of them familiar enough to need no documentation and little exposition. One is that the pericope represents an interpolation, a later addition. But this leaves the question of motive still unanswered. The most popular explanation identifies the young man of the incident with Mark himself; the author included the story because it happened to *him*. But this is likely to seem on reflection too personal and accidental an explanation—out of keeping with what we may gather as to the serious purpose of the author in his Gospel, and especially in the Passion section of it. Besides, does not Papias tell us that Mark "neither heard the Lord nor followed him"? [1] The third explanation is that the little story was created (or at least was deemed important enough to be remembered) on the basis of Amos 2:16 and Gen. 39:12. "The messianic interpretation of Amos 2:16 may have suggested the entire incident," writes Montefiore,[2] who goes on to quote Klostermann as saying that "the gospel story teller apparently wished to enrich the whole environment (*Umgebung*) of Jesus with a prophetic meaning." The main difficulty remains— the irrelevance of the pericope. This difficulty is less serious when the passage is taken symbolically (i.e., in connection with Amos 2:16) than when understood as the intrusion of a merely personal experience; but the proposed symbolic meaning is not closely related to the Passion.

In a footnote in my book, *Christ the Lord*,[3] I ventured to make a suggestion which perhaps deserves a somewhat fuller statement. It would appear that Mark likes to describe events in proleptic fashion, or at any rate to make cryptic references to coming future events. There is no resurrection appearance in Mark, but many find in the transfiguration scene an unmistakable anticipation of such an appearance. The Passion story ends with some women coming to anoint the body of Jesus and being unable to do so because the body is gone, but the Passion story begins (Mark

---

[1] Eusebius, *Church History*, iii, 39, 15. Cf. Frederick C. Grant, *The Earliest Gospel* (New York and Nashville: Abingdon-Cokesbury Press, 1943), pp. 52–53.

[2] *The Synoptic Gospels* (London: Macmillan & Co., 1927), Vol. I, pp. 349–50.

[3] Chicago: Willett, Clark, 1945, p. 100.

14:1 f.) with the account of another woman breaking on him "an alabaster box of ointment . . . very precious," while Jesus says of her: "She has done what she could [and what her sisters later could not]; she has anointed me beforehand for the burying." Is it then too fanciful to suggest that this apparently whimsical story of the young man and the linen cloth got into the gospel tradition because Mark, or some early community, saw in it an anticipation of the empty tomb, with which this Gospel culminates? Just as the young man escaped, leaving only the linen cloth with which he was covered, so Jesus, "seized" (the same Greek word is used in vv. 46, 49, and 51) also on that same occasion, was likewise destined to escape the hands of his enemies, leaving only the linen cloth with which he was wrapped. We note in Mark 15:46 that Jesus' body before burial was wrapped in such a cloth (σινδών). Although Mark does not refer to the cloth as left in the tomb in 16:1–8, this omission is not at all decisive; Mark depended a great deal upon the discernment of his readers. For example, there is no reference to 14:3 ff. in 16:1–8 (even different Greek words are used for the act and the material of the anointing); but can there be any doubt that Mark wants his readers to remember at 16:1 that Jesus has already been "anointed . . . beforehand for the burying"? (One can but wonder about a possible connection between the young man clothed [νεανίσκος . . . περιβεβλημένος] in the linen cloth in 14:51–52 and the young man clothed [νεανίσκον . . . περιβεβλημέ-νον] in a white robe in 16:5.)

We know that this idea of the linen cloth (whether σινδών, ὀθόνιον, or some other synonym) as being alone left after Jesus' resurrection had some importance in the tradition. Note John 20:5–7 and the following passage from the Acts of Pilate 15:6: "and I [Joseph of Arimathea] said unto him: 'Who art thou, Lord?' And he said unto me: 'I am Jesus, whose body thou didst beg of Pilate, and didst clothe in clean linen and cover my face with a napkin, and lay me in thy new cave and roll a great stone upon the door of the cave.' And I said to him that spake with me: 'Show me the place where I laid thee.' And he brought me and showed me the place where I laid him, and the linen cloth lay therein, and the napkin that was upon his face." [4] More important is a passage from the Gospel according to the Hebrews as quoted by Jerome: "Now the Lord [after the resurrection], when he had given the linen cloth unto the servant of the priest, went unto James and appeared to him. . . ." [5]

This suggestion is offered merely as an additional possible way of interpreting a passage whose presence in the tradition is difficult to explain, however it is interpreted.

It may be finally noted that the interpretations favored of the transfiguration and the anointing at Bethany, as well as the proposed interpretation of Mark 14:51–52, strongly support the view that Mark originally ended and was intended to end at 16:8.

[4] Translation from Montague Rhodes James, *The Apocryphal New Testament* (Oxford: Clarendon Press, 1924), p. 111.

[5] *Of Illustrious Men* 2; translation by M. R. James, *ibid.*, pp. 3–4. Note that there is also a reference to the "servant of the high priest" in the context of our passage, Mark 14:47.

Community in the Synoptic Gospels

by HOLT H. GRAHAM
Seabury-Western Theological Seminary

This essay is an attempt to delineate the earliest Christian community, using the Synoptic Gospels as source material. Our premise is that the form and character of the community express primary assumptions about common life which Jesus and his first followers inherited from Hebrew culture. That is to say that the assumptions are not consciously made or chosen. They are of the order of underlying assumptions given in a culture, accepted as a matter of course by most of those born in it, and expressing themselves in the "way of life" of a society.

Christianity began within Palestinian Judaism. The character of the first Christian community is determined, on our premise, by the assumptions about common life made in Israel and in Judaism. We shall accordingly indicate briefly what these are as modern scholarship understands them, and then look to the Synoptic Gospels for evidences of their expression. The first section will be very brief; for further information the reader is referred to J. Pedersen: *Israel, Its Life and Culture*, Part II, upon which the following account is based; W. Eichrodt: *Theologie des Alten Testaments*, and L. Baeck: *The Essence of Judaism*.

I. COMMUNITY AND ITS TYPES IN THE OLD TESTAMENT

For the Israelite, community is the unquestioned presupposition of all life. The power and extent of this feeling for community comes as a shock to the Western mind, for the Israelite assumption is the reverse of that which understands society as an aggregate of individuals from whom its life and meaning is derived. There is indeed no word in English that adequately conveys what the Israelite understands by community. All life is common life, and the common life has its roots in the divine. This is to say that all life is understood religiously. The primary fact is the relation between God and the People, understood as a totality. This explains not only the phenomena of early Israelite history, but also the perhaps even more remarkable story of Judaism, in which the rise of individualism, the vicissitudes of history, the development of personal religion, and the growth of eschatology have the character and effect they do because of the persistence of the sense of community.

For the Israelite, a community is a totality which he calls *shalom* (peace). The word "peace" indicates a psychic unity, a harmony of souls who share a common blessing. The soul in turn is an entirety with a definite stamp (body is a weak manifestation of soul). Man did not receive a *nephesh* (soul) in the Genesis account, he *became* one. This entirety may be called *lebh* (heart) if one is thinking of character and operating power, or *ruach* (spirit) if one has in view what we call will (for which Hebrew has no separate word), or the soul as a willing agent. And because the soul is so understood, community implies a harmony of will, and is in danger of or in process of dissolution when strife between brethren arises. Further, harmony of will is achieved not by agreement as we understand it, but when the impress of the strongest soul in the community is received upon the heart of the others and all wills are conformed to his, becoming one will. A community in peace has one heart, one will, one soul. It is a psychic unity.

Community exhibits two main types: Family and Covenant. Over the community of the family we need not linger, except to call to mind some examples of its unity (or "peace"). The crime of Achan (Josh. 7, recalled in I Chron. 2:7) brings guilt upon his whole house; the entire households of Dathan and Abiram are swallowed up by the earth because of their rebellion against Moses (Num. 16, recalled in Deut. 11:6); David's house rises with him (II Sam. 7:16; I Kgs. 12:26) and is stricken with him for his crime against Uriah (II Sam. 12:10); Eli is implicated in the ruin of his sons (II Sam. 2:27 ff.). The family has one will and therefore a common responsibility; the visitation of punishment upon the third and fourth generations may be a shock to the Western mind, but it is not to the Israelite, for within the psychic unity of a father's house there is no point in distinguishing what is done by any one generation.

The strangeness of this view increases rather than lessens as we pass from the family community to the community of the covenant type. As one might expect, communities of covenant are as a rule not as strong as the family, and according to Israelite morality obligations of blood come first: "There is no other blessing and honor than the one a man has with his family, and no obligation can clash with that of the claim of kindred, because this is the deepest of all." [1] However, the covenant of unrelated persons can be so strong that the community of family gives way before it, as in the case of the friendship of David and Jonathan. A further illustration of the overruling power of covenant is the story of Jacob and Esau in Genesis 32. By virtue of his acceptance of Jacob's gifts, Esau entered into covenant with him, and had therefore to forego vengeance or any claims upon Jacob whatsoever.

[1] J. Pedersen, *Israel, Its Life and Culture*, p. 282. (London: Oxford University Press. Copenhagen: Branner og Korchs Forlag.)

Without going into further detail, we now attempt certain generalizations about communities of covenant, whether of friendship, alliance, or discipleship. A community of covenant is a unity of souls and therefore a harmony of wills excluding the possibility of essential points of conflict. The covenant creates a new community-will which changes individual wills. This does not imply equality within the covenant community, for the center of gravity is nearer the strong soul than the weaker. On the other hand, the will is common to all, and so the covenant is symbolized in some token external to but common to the community. This pledge may be an object such as a heap of stones (Gen. 31:46) or an altar (Gen. 33:20), or an act such as a handshake (Job 17:3). The more solemn covenant is symbolized in the rite of the common meal [2] which is given by the greater (Gen. 26:30) who accordingly sits in the father's place, the place of honor.

Finally, the covenant is the presupposition of all life, and so is a holy thing and has its roots in the divine powers. All life is common life, and the law of love for one's neighbor is not a dogmatic invention, but a direct expression of the character of soul. The law of love to God is likewise the natural expression of the soul of the Israelite community whose life was constituted in him. It was constituted also by him: his call, his covenant, his love. He is the initiator of a covenant which binds them to him and him to them whether in peace or in the discord that means the dissolution of Israel's life.

We must now say a word about one particular form of community, that of rabbi and disciples. There is no explicit reference to this in the Old Testament (except the passing one in Isa. 8:16), but it is common enough in the life of Judaism.

> Every Jewish teacher had a group of students who lived with him, attended to his needs, and accompanied him wherever he went; these were known as his "disciples" ("learners"). Or, since

[2] I Kgs. 13; Ps. 41:10; II Sam. 3:30; Ex. 4:14; Num. 18:19; II Chron. 13:5.

they always walked behind him, they were also said to "come after him" or "follow him." Jesus' summons, "Follow me," was therefore a call to discipleship in a similar sense; whoever obeyed the summons must give up his former life, in order to serve Jesus and to learn from him.[3]

It is from this point that we proceed to an examination of the idea of community in the Synoptic Gospels.

II. THE COMMUNITY OF RABBI AND DISCIPLES

The community of Jesus and his disciples is inaugurated with the call of the first disciples (Peter, Andrew, James, and John, Mark 1:16–20, Matt. 4:18–22) who are summoned with the technical words "follow me." So also is Levi in Mark 2:14 and parallels. The weight and seriousness of this call are indicated by the fact that James and John leave their father to join themselves to Jesus; the same aspect of the relationship is indicated in the words of Jesus in Mark 3:31–45, Matt. 12:46–50, Luke 8:19–20, where the community of those who hear the word (will) of God and do it is set above Jesus' family ties, and in the words of Matt. 10:37–38, Luke 14:25–27, where love of the Rabbi is set above love of family as a condition of discipleship. Likewise in Mark 8:19–23, Luke 9:57–62,[4] those who would "follow" must be prepared to share the master's homelessness and obey with the unquestioning alacrity that does not even pause to bury the dead or say good-by to one's family, and irrevocably renounces all things in favor of discipleship (Luke 14:28–33, on the cost of discipleship). Conversely, disloyalty to one's master is a terrible crime, as is evidenced by the remorse of Peter (Mark 14:72 and parallels) and the suicide of Judas (Matt. 27:3–10).

Once the relationship has been established, the disciples are henceforth identified by their relationship to their Rabbi, as John's

[3] B. S. Easton, *What Jesus Taught*, p. 106.
[4] These words, however, probably belong to a section on the Kingdom and community.

are by their relationship to him,[5] and when their conduct comes under attack the accusers apply to the master and he defends his own.[6] These are not the casual followers, but those who have accepted the strict terms of discipleship as set forth in Matt. 10:37–38, in Luke 14:25–27 (the conditions of discipleship), and in Matt. 8:19–22, Luke 9:57–62 (two claimants to discipleship).[7]

The summary account of the call of the Twelve in Mark 3:13–19 includes notice of the disciples' receipt of authority from their master to preach and to cast out demons. This derivative authority, theirs by virtue of discipleship, is illustrated in the Mission of the Twelve [8] and in the description of their work in Mark 6:12–13, Luke 9:6; but it is clear that though they share their master's power, their share is less than his,[9] for he succeeds where they had failed in healing the epileptic boy. What the disciples are to preach by virtue of the power given them is carefully taught them, and they share as others do not in the teaching. So the many notices of Jesus' explaining things to them "privately" or "when they were in the house" or "afterward"; [10] and in Mark 9:30 the very presence of Jesus and his disciples is not to be noised abroad, for he is teaching them about the destiny of the Son of Man.

Those who have accepted the solemn call to discipleship and entered into this covenant relationship are, as we should expect, bound up in a unity with their master. This is indicated in the narrative of the Confession of Peter at Caesarea Philippi (Mark 8:27–33 and parallels), where the overtone of the prediction of the sufferings is the implication that the disciples will share the fate

[5] Mark 2:18–20 and parallels; Matt. 11:2–6; Luke 7:18–23.

[6] Mark 2:16 ff. and parallels; Mark 7:1–23; Matt. 15:1–20.

[7] Contents of citations are indicated by the titles given them in Huck's *Synopsis.*

[8] Mark 6:6b–11; Matt. 10:1, 5–16; Luke 11:1–12.

[9] Mark 9:18, 28; Matt. 17:16, 19; Luke 9:40.

[10] Mark 4:11, 34; 7:17–23; Matt. 15:12–19; Mark 9:9; Matt. 17:9; Mark 13:3; Mark 10:32–34; Matt. 20:17–19; Luke 18:31–34; Matt. 26:1–5; Mark 14:14, etc.

of their master. This may well reflect the life of the later brother-hood; [11] but even if there is a reading back, the notion of a common destiny is not foreign to the character of discipleship. The same note is present in the prediction of the Passion in Mark 10:32–34, where the marks of the disciple-master covenant are present in the words "going before," "follow," and in Jesus' taking the Twelve aside to instruct them. Likewise in the narrative of Gethsemane (Mark 14:32–42 and parallels) three of the disciples are instructed, "Abide ye here, and watch with me." [12] Finally, the same unity is illustrated in the fact that the disciples are identified with Jesus in the words of Luke 10:16, "He that heareth you heareth me; and he that rejecteth you rejecteth me; and he that rejecteth me rejecteth him that sent me." [13]

We noted in the first section that covenants of the more solemn type were marked by the rite of a common meal. The Last Supper is such a meal, the solemn type of previous frequent meals. So Jesus must, in the words of the Gospels, eat his last Passover with the Twelve. I think we need not labor this, and it is expedient at this point to pass to the idea of community as held by the Christian brotherhood,[14] for the words, "This is my blood of the covenant [Luke, new covenant in my blood] which is poured out for many," lead us necessarily to a consideration of the wider community.

The words "for many," taken with the saying, "If any man should follow me," addressed to the multitude in Mark 8:34–9:1 and parallels, present us with an alternative: either we have here a radical extension of the discipleship covenant made by Jesus

[11] "Brotherhood" refers to post-Resurrection community—cf. J. Wach, *Sociology of Religion*, Pt. II, ch. V, secs. 6, 7.

[12] The presence of only three of the Twelve does not affect the argument: for, since the disciples are one body, the part equals the whole. So in the story of the Confession of Peter, he is in that moment the Church; and in Matt. 18:20 the local congregation acts with the authority of the whole Church.

[13] Same with variations in Matt. 10:39–42; Mark 9:37 and parallels.

[14] See note 11, above.

himself, or else we have the conceptions of the evangelists, which is to say a reflection of the experience of the Church. On the latter view, the narratives of the Feeding of the Multitude represent the same extension of the covenant, and are a type of the covenant-meals of the Christian community. If on the other hand the extension of the community is held to be the work of Jesus himself (it is the proper work of disciples to make disciples), the Feeding narratives do not come into the discussion, for the multitudes did not enter the disciples' community.

Here one must introduce a qualification that applies to much of the foregoing discussion. There is no doubt that the life and thought of the Christian community of the post-Resurrection period determines both the form and the selection of much of the Synoptic material. One's decision about the authenticity of sayings and the accuracy of narratives, based upon critical study, will affect the assignment of evidence to the foregoing or following parts of this discussion. However, the organic relation of the community of disciples to the community of the brotherhood enable one to make some generalizations about the life of the former based upon deductions from the record left by the latter. This is the assumption and principle, whether the application of it above be accurate or not.

III. THE BROTHERHOOD

We turn, then, to certain passages in the Synoptics which seem quite clearly to reflect the life of the Christian brotherhood, the larger community of the New Covenant of which the blood of Christ is the token as the blood of the Sinai sacrifice was of the Old (Ex. 24:6–8). We notice first of all in the Beatitudes a change of person from "they" to "ye" in Matt. 5:11. They seem at first sight to be a special word to the disciples, but in view of Luke's usage and the emphasis of Matthew elsewhere, it would seem that Matt. 5:11–12 reflects the life of the Christian brotherhood which in its own time shared in the sufferings of its Lord.[15] The community of sufferings and the requirement of loyalty placed upon those who would be of this covenant is reflected in the warnings following the similes of salt and light (Matt. 5:13; Luke 11:33, 14:34–35) and that of the saying, "Not everyone that saith unto me Lord, Lord, etc.," in Matt. 7:21–23; Luke 6:46, 13:26–27, which are the negative side of the saying cited above to the effect that they are Jesus' brethren who do the will of God.

Certainly we are confronted with the life of the brotherhood in such a passage as Mark 4:13–20 and parallels, where an explanation of the Parable of the Sower is given. To begin with, a Jewish parable is effectively turned into the allegory form more congenial to the Hellenistic mind, and the background one may assume for the latter is not the life of the disciples. Rather, we have here a different situation, with the immediate covenant of rabbi and disciples replaced by a diffused community into which potential members fail to enter because they fail to accept one of the terms of the covenant, i.e., obedience and fidelity to the Risen Lord. Again and again the disciples "did not understand," to be sure, but despite the failure of Judas and the lapse of Peter, their community was not marked by the brokenness implied in the Matthaean form of the parable of the wheat and the tares (13:24–30, 36–43), where what is in Mark 4:26–29 a parable of the Kingdom is clearly applied to the Church. The internal life of the Church is again reflected in the Matthaean version of the Confession of Peter in the 16th chapter, which establishes by a word from the Lord the status and authority of the Apostle;[16] and in Matt. 18:15–20, where the authority of the Church to bind and to loose is stated (and note

[15] Cf. Rom. 8:17; II Cor. 1:5; II Tim. 2:11; I Pet. 2:21, 4:13, 4:16, 5:10, etc.

[16] It is instructive in this connection to refer to Acts 11:1–18, where Peter defends before the church in Jerusalem his action in baptizing Cornelius. He raises no question about their right to an accounting. The authority of the apostle is integral to the mutual interdependence characteristic of the "peace" (*shalom*) of the community.

that the part has the power of the whole), and where its status is defined in a manner parallel to the identity of disciples with their master discussed above (vs. 20). The same possession of derivative or shared authority is of course stated in the commission of Matt. 28:16–20.

A final panel in our picture of the life of the brotherhood is found in two interesting sets of parallels: Matt. 10:17–25 = Luke 12:11–12 and Mark 13:9–13 = Matt. 14:9–14 = Luke 21:12–19. The first contains the instructions given by Jesus ostensibly to his disciples—"Ye shall not have gone through the cities of Israel, till the Son of man be come"—but which accurately describe the persecutions of the later Church and set a premium upon perseverance to the end. The second passage is in the apocalyptic discourse, and in it Mark and Luke give the description of persecution placed by Matthew in the first. Here again we have the community of suffering shared by Lord and Church, with the sharpness of division between the Church and the World indicated by the prediction that brethren will be delivered up by members of their own families. It is in this context that I should place the saying of Matt. 10:32–33 = Luke 12:8–9, "Every one therefore who shall confess me before men, etc."

In summary, what we find in those passages which reflect the life of the brotherhood is a larger covenant community sharing the life of its Lord ("There am I in the midst of them," Matt. 18:20) and his sufferings, sharing in his power and authority, sharply distinguished from those outside it, continuing the covenant-meal ("as oft as ye shall drink it"), and united in a bond stronger than natural ties ("brother shall deliver up brother and father child and child father").

IV. The Kingdom and the Community

We shall conclude with some remarks about community as made by the Kingdom of God; but these will be fragmentary, for to say anything definite about the nature of such community would presuppose a study of the relation of Church and Kingdom far beyond the scope of this paper. We may say one or two things, however.

That the Kingdom of God does create a community not co-extensive with the community of disciples seems to be indicated in two passages. The first is Mark 9:38–41 = Luke 9:49–50, where it is said of the strange wonderworker, "He that is not against us is for us," and where the disciples are told not to forbid him even though he is not "of us." (Matthew, who probably identifies Church and Kingdom, reverses the saying.) The second is Matt. 11:12 = Luke 16:16, where it is said that from the days of John the Baptist people have been entering the Kingdom. Other passages which may be considered under this head are Matt. 8:5–13, Luke 7:1–10, 13:28–30, where after the healing of the centurion's servant it is said that many shall come from the East and the West to sit down in the Kingdom (i.e., at the Messianic banquet—many from East and West may of course mean the Church); and the parable of the Messianic Feast in Matt. 22:1–14 = Luke 14:15–24. Of the many passages where a relationship between discipleship (or membership in the brotherhood) and place in the Kingdom is stated or implied, we may select one not yet cited: in Mark 10:17–31, Matt. 19:16–30, Luke 18:18–30, 22:28–30, the Rich Young Ruler who cannot meet the test of discipleship has thereby missed entering the Kingdom.

This study is incomplete because we have put to one side not only the question of Kingdom and Community, but also because we have not considered certain other aspects, chief among which is the community as eschatological.[17] Nevertheless, we have perhaps delineated or indicated three main ideas of community presented in the Synoptic Gospels. The first is the covenant community of

[17] See F. C. Grant, *An Introduction to New Testament Thought*, 1950, pp. 268–270.

Jesus and his disciples inaugurated by their call, symbolized in the rite of a common meal, and evincing the characteristics of psychic unity and wholeness we should expect on Hebraic presuppositions. The second is the covenant community of the brotherhood. As Israel was a holy community because it had its roots in the divine life of the God of the Covenant, so the brotherhood is a holy community with its roots in the life of the living Lord Christ, sharing in his life and deriving its character, status, and meaning from that relationship. The third is the community of the Kingdom of God, with which we have not attempted to deal.

WORKS CITED

Joh. Pedersen, *Israel, Its Life and Culture*. Parts I–II, Eng. tr., Copenhagen: Branner; London: Oxford, 1926.

Joachim Wach, *The Sociology of Religion*. Chicago: Univ. of Chicago Press, 1944.

B. S. Easton, *What Jesus Taught*. New York: Abingdon Press, 1938.

A. Huck–H. Lietzmann, *A Synopsis of the First Three Gospels*. English ed. by F. L. Cross. Tübingen: Mohr, 1936.

W. Eichrodt, *Theologie des Alten Testaments*. Berlin: Evangelische Verlagsanstalt, Teil I, dritte Auflage; Teile II u. III, zweite Auflage, 1948.

F. C. Grant, *An Introduction to New Testament Thought*, New York: Abingdon-Cokesbury, 1950.

SEE IN ADDITION

George Johnston, *The Doctrine of the Church in the New Testament*. Cambridge Univ. Press, 1943.

K. L. Schmidt, *The Church*. Trans. from Kittel. *Theologisches Wörterbuch zum Neuen Testament*, by J. R. Coates. London: A. and C. Black, 1950.

Overconversion in Paul's Churches

by HENRY J. CADBURY
Harvard University

Naturally one thinks of conversion to religion as a transition performed in a rectilinear direction. This may be gradual, the convert slowly sloughing off old thoughts and practices for new ones. It may also be rapid, seemingly instantaneous. For the latter process the apostle Paul is the classic example as represented, perhaps misrepresented, in the Acts of the Apostles. His letters, while they neither confirm nor refute this idea for himself, suggest a less simple view of the process in his converts.

The modern religious group to which I belong has for many generations maintained its membership primarily from those born and reared under its influence. Distinct from these "birthright members" there are new adherents for whose transition our traditional word is "convinced." Some recent wag, observing the tendency with which some of these latter outstrip the former in rigor, has coined the word "overconvinced." They are overconvinced Quakers. It is for a phenomenon of this kind that I would use the term "overconversion."

The letters of Paul indicate a like feature in the churches that he addressed, especially those churches which he himself planted and to which he was writing shortly afterward.[1] What he so generally seems to correct is not partial conversion but an excess of change. The seventeenth-century term "Halfway Covenant" would have had no meaning for him or for his converts, whether Jew or Gentile. Neither would our contemporary term, "semi-convert," apply.

The Gentiles, whom he considered especially his parish, were called by him to radical change, and it would not be surprising if they needed egging on from a halting acceptance of the gospel to a more complete conversion. Yet of one of Paul's earliest letters, now lost, we know that it produced people who construed his demands as complete separation of believers from unbelievers.[2] His answer is that their position expects too much rather than too little. Presumably what was involved here was some matter of sex, an area where the Corinthian standards were traditionally low. A few paragraphs later he discusses problems of marriage. Readers of I Corinthians 7 often feel—and women are particularly sensitive here—that Paul is radically opposing marriage and that he makes a few grudging concessions on its behalf. Whether Paul is to be regarded as "anti-feminist" depends on what was the view of those whom he was answering. Indeed, he must always be appraised in the light of the circumstances, and these are not always known. Otherwise his demands will be treated as concessions, his liberalism as conservatism, his modesty as pride, and *vice versa*. In reality some Corinthians might have been pressing the celibate view, while Paul, without offending them, points out that marriages ought not to be lightly terminated. Even Christians married to non-Christians should not take the initiative at separation, but should welcome their opportunity to benefit spiritually both the spouse and the children. The strict adherents of the curious spiritual mar-

[1] Thessalonica, Galatia, and Corinth. For Philippi the interval between foundation and epistle is usually regarded as longer.
[2] I Cor. 5:9. Some have thought II Cor. 6:14–7:1 is an actual fragment of this letter.

riages mentioned later in the chapter, where love was expected to remain Platonic, are reminded that there is no sin in transferring to the normal married relation.

Indeed, other reactions to Paul indicate that he again and again has to deal with positions which though more extreme than his own were naturally arrived at by converts who tended to be over-converted. The taboo of idolatry, indeed, of everything connected with paganism, would be part of Paul's message to the Gentiles. At Thessalonica he had told them to turn to God from idols. Taking this literally, some Corinthian converts evidently went so far as to condemn the eating of food that, having once been offered to idols, had come into the general meat supply and might seem to have lost thereby, when eaten at a non-religious meal, all taint of idolatry. Paul's problem is in part created by the rigorists—his own word is "the weak"—who are inconveniently sensitive not only about eating such food themselves but also about other Christians who quite unsuspectingly may do so. But the other group, "the strong," may equally be regarded as extremists who cited Paul on their side. As Jew or Christian, Paul regarded pagan gods as nothing more than their idols and their idols as nothing more than the stuff they were made of. To make little of any asso-ciation with idols, as "the strong" in Corinth did, might seem a legitimate extension of Paul's teaching. His letter deals faithfully with them also, both for their own sake and for the sake of "the weak."

It is not necessary to list other features of Paul's teaching which, just because they were new to Gentiles, lent themselves to being taken overseriously. In the area of belief Paul, the ex-Pharisee, more than ever now as a Christian believed and taught the doctrine of resurrection and, indeed, the whole eschatological program of Judaism, including the eager expectation [3] of the

[3] The other half of the passage quoted above would better be translated "and to expect his Son from heaven" than with the English verb "wait for."

parousia. For most Gentiles such ideas were novel and exciting. They easily went too far and expected it too early. Instead of too little and too late, their messianic hope was too much and too soon. Paul's warning that other things must happen first is parallel to other New Testament passages. Evidently elsewhere, as well as in Thessalonica, the apocalyptic hope was interpreted prematurely.

The idlers in that church are often associated with this same overexpectancy. Indifference to the acquisition of even a modest personal income might have arisen from this source logically, but Paul makes no such connection and millennialists are not always logical. Did Paul or others say at Thessalonica some things about the moral perils of wealth or about the merits of voluntary poverty, like some words we find in the other letters and in the gospels? Certainly he claimed to be as content with want as with abundance. The overemphasis on such teaching could quite as easily make some converts what we should call economically irresponsible. In either case the idlers had gone beyond what Paul had intended rather than fallen short of it.

The problem of Galatians is similar in that here also two solutions are possible. Professor Ropes once called it a singular problem; I would call it a plural problem, and our uncertainty is probably due to the dual situation and to the polarity of Paul's own mind. But looked at simply, the Christianity to which the Galatian Gentiles first adhered under Paul's preaching overlapped contemporary Judaism very extensively in theology and in ethics. Paul's preaching and especially his practice may have set no clear limits before them. Some of these adherents might well feel that they should accept still more Judaism than when they had first believed, and evidently they were encouraged in this feeling by some newer arrivals among them, who recommended circumcision, sabbath observance, and the like. If, however, one looks from a different angle at the gospel that Paul preached it had a flavor of moral self-determination which easily moved towards antinomianism. Apparently in both directions the overconverted were not without excuse in Paul. Were the unveiled women worshippers in Corinth or those who were boastful about scandalous behavior merely transferring Paul's own libertarianism into license? Did they claim to be remembering Paul in everything and maintaining the traditions he delivered?

To judge from his letters Paul's mind was antithetic in structure just as his speech tends to elaborated antithesis. Such a temperament does not readily emphasize the golden mean,[4] and such a preacher is sure to make some converts who are more radical than himself. Like Marcion long after, they were more Pauline than Paul. One may say that in I Corinthians Paul displays an irenic attitude. In chapter 12 he seems to take a neutral stand towards alternative forms of vocal participation in worship. Superficially that is true. He seems in chapter 1 to be calling off his own partisans as well as those of Apollos or Cephas. Whether in the matter of parties or of the several gifts of the Spirit, he begins in a liberal and nonpartisan way, only to end with a strongly expressed preference. Even in his own case moderation proves to have not the last word, and much more so in his converts. Almost none of the polemic of Paul's letters is directed at non-Christians. In longer and shorter passages he is criticizing Christian converts. Like other teachers he faces the problem of pupils overdoing his own viewpoint.

Another instance is the obscure situation in II Corinthians 1–7. Paul had written an interim letter in order that as he says "your zeal for us might be revealed to you in the sight of God." But now that he is satisfied on this point he urges them to forgive and com-

[4] This Aristotelian ethical conception was not unknown in Paul's time, but it seems unlikely that he preached it at the start, or even warned against being "righteous overmuch" (Scotch "unco guid"). Possibly, as has been suggested (*Theologische Literaturzeitung* 75 [1950], 506 ff.), at I Cor. 4:6 he used the phrase μὴ ὑπέρ as a slogan like μηδὲν ἄγαν, *ne quid nimis*.

fort the offender instead of extending his punishment. He is afraid
they will be too zealous.

Some overconversion may have been merely a pose, or an argument adopted by skeptical converts to produce a *reductio ad ab-
surdum*. One suspects that the objection of some Corinthians to
belief in the resurrection of Christians was that it was untrue because it was unthinkable. "How are the dead raised? With what
kind of body do they come?" are objections rather than real in-
quiries. The Sadducees' question in the Gospels about the woman
married in turn to seven brothers was likewise intended to discredit a belief by applying it. Those in Corinth who had taken
Paul's teaching of bodily resurrection too literally were not
friendly converts, but evidently they bothered his friends who did
not recognize that Paul's teaching was being overpressed. Those
who said Paul's doctrine of separateness from the world was im-
practical may have been in the same situation. But whether they
acted "from good will" or "from envy and rivalry," their gospel
was Paul's gospel overdone.

While much that I have said is generally accepted, when taken
all together it supplies a pattern that should be borne in mind in
judging the problem of Paul's mission as a whole. I will not say
that those who heard Paul either came away unconverted or were
overconverted; inevitably some that Paul reached moved only
slowly and slightly towards his real standard for them. They slid
back and needed to be prodded on. From reports received and
from his general experience he included in his letters exhortations
to stand fast and to progress. Yet quite often his advice and his
reminder of what he had previously stood for by word or deed is
intended for those who go too far. His example of celibacy is not
to be taken as universal. His own industry at his handicraft belies
any suggestion of an ideal of freedom from labor. His unconcern
about baptizing people himself likewise answers the invidious
claims of his overloyal partisans. Not that what he had done and

said was at the time intended to meet such unexpected developments; they were natural expressions of his faith. They seemed later to have been misunderstood or overlooked. It was not immodest in Paul under such circumstances to call attention to his own practice.

Much remains obscure in that half-lost interchange represented in Paul's genuine letters. Yet in dealing with the obscurities it will always be well to remember that quite likely Paul is thinking not of the underconverted but of the overconverted, as is evident in the less obscure passages. In so far as his work eventuated in a Christianity as wholesome as his own it had often to swing back from excesses made in spite of him but under his influence. Perhaps that is one reason why his influence in the generations that immediately followed him is so hard to trace. It depended on the stabilization of a pendulum. Reactions, echoes, results following from him, all are claimed by historians, but very little authentic and specific Paulinism is proved.

The feature of overconversion is probably not unusual in religion. Theophrastus in his *Character of a Superstitious Man*, Lucian in his story of *Proteus Peregrinus*, both seem by caricature to hint at excessive expression of religious loyalty. The early Christians themselves noted that proselytes to Judaism turned out to be—I soften the expression—"twofold more" Jewish than ordinary Jews.[5] This tendency of converts has been mentioned here as one clue to the understanding of Paul's letters and his churches. It may also have some bearing on the understanding of Paul. Perhaps his personality tended to release an overdose, and to put him constantly on the defensive. His adherents by their very zeal were an embarrassment to him. This situation may account for the alternation he shows between extreme statement and caution, between partisanship and conciliation. It is only another facet of what has well been called his prismatic personality.

[5] Matt. 23:15; Justin, *Dialogue with Trypho*, 122:2.

Whether overconversion to Christianity is much of a feature of modern times is a different question. New fashions of scholarship and of theology have their overzealous devotees, but the simple gospel is rarely taken in overdose. More characteristic is perhaps the opposite phenomenon, by which Christianity in some very mild form, traditional, ritual, or rational, acts like inoculation to prevent the recipient from ever succumbing to the full rigor of conversion. For it is as possible to be inoculated against good as against evil.

The Wisdom of the Corinthians

by ROBERT M. GRANT
University of the South

In I Corinthians 1:22 the apostle Paul says that "Greeks seek wisdom," and he immediately contrasts with their search the Christian preaching of Christ crucified. The first four chapters of his letter are devoted to a vigorous attack on their wisdom and, above all, on their idea that they themselves are wise. Commentators have long been aware that the Corinthians' self-esteem is related to the Stoic-Cynic ideal of the wise man, but they have not fully appreciated the extent to which this ideal permeated their thought.

Every virtue was ascribed to the wise man, who alone led his life in accordance with reason. He was not deceived and did not deceive; he did all things well; he was not affected by evil; he was happy, rich, handsome, free, the only true king. Since reason instructed him, he was the only good man. "All things are rightly said to be his, since he alone knows how to use all things" (Cicero, *De fin.* iii. 75; cf. 1 Cor. 3:21–22).[1]

The ideal of the wise man permeated Stoic thought, even though it was often criticized by other schools which asked for even one example of such a person (Cicero, *Lucullus* 145, with Reid's note).

[1] For a full discussion cf. M. Pohlenz, *Die Stoa* (Göttingen, 1948), I, 153–58.

By Porphyry's time (*De abstinentia* iii. 3) Stoics held that there had been one or two such men, but no more.

Certain Corinthian Christians believed that they belonged to the select group of the wise men. Since they were wise, all things were theirs (I Cor. 3:21; *Stoicorum veterum fragmenta*, ed. von Arnim, III 590, 591). They were truly rich (4:8; SVF III 594, 595, etc.); they were truly kings (SVF III 599, etc.). Because they were wise they were "perfect" (2:6; SVF I 566), powerful (1:26; SVF III 567), well-born (1:26; SVF III 594, 597, 603), prudent (4:10; SVF III 655), and held in honor (4:10; SVF III 603). They may have regarded themselves as proficient in rhetoric because of their wisdom (1:20, etc.; SVF III 654, 655).

The wise man will live in accordance with nature. Thus certain Corinthians apparently argued that since "meats were for the belly, and the belly for meats," any sexual relationships which seemed natural were therefore permissible (6:13). Precisely the same line of argument was upheld by the Cynic Diogenes (Diogenes Laertius vi. 46), who was followed by the older cynicizing Stoa (SVF III 743–746). In this way it was possible to justify incest (I Cor. 5:1, with Weiss's note), which could be regarded as a proof of the wise man's freedom from convention. The wise man alone is truly free and has absolute freedom of action (cf. SVF III 355). These Corinthians could say, "Everything is permissible for me," just as a Stoic wise man could say it (I Cor. 6:12; Musonius Rufus, frag. 31, p. 122 Hense).

Paul's reply is essentially based on the primacy of revelation, but it makes use of several philosophical themes. For example, he points out the fact that the Corinthians are not really wise, powerful, and well-born (1:26). Similarly the skeptics argued that since there is no such things as the Stoic wise man, all men are fools (Sextus Empiricus, *Adv. math.* vii. 432). He calls attention to the fact that as an apostle he has actually suffered hunger and thirst and punishment and fatigue (4:11–13). A somewhat similar criticism is found in Cicero (*Lucullus* 135, with Reid's note). The Stoic ideal is unreal. Paul admits that all things are permissible (here his own ideal of freedom is coördinate with that of the Stoics), but he insists with the later Stoa that not all things are profitable (6:12). The apostle did not need to study philosophy in order to make use of these themes, for they were common property in his day. Nevertheless, they are philosophical themes.

Other Christians at Corinth wrote him a letter in which they asked his advice or support in certain problems within the community. They were upholding the ideal of continence (7:1), an ideal which he largely shared. They were arguing that they could eat meats offered to idols because idols were nothing (8:1). They said, "All of us have knowledge," but they meant (as Paul seems to point out, 8:7) that some of them had knowledge while others had not.[2] They claimed to possess special spiritual gifts, the highest of which was prophecy, which they identified with glossolalia. The apostle makes use of the Stoic idea of the body and its members (cf. W. L. Knox in *Journal of Theological Studies* 39, 1938, 243–46) and explains that true prophecy is not identical with, but superior to, talking in tongues (12:12–28; 14). He stresses the superiority of Christian love to glossolalia, prophecy, knowledge, and communism (13:1–3). Either this group or some other group insisted that there is no resurrection of the dead (15:12) and asked the skeptical question of the kind of body which could rise (15:35).

Within Judaism or a community related to Judaism the ideal of absolute continence is strange. As Weiss observes (*Komm.*, 170) the Old Testament says not "it is good for a man not to touch a woman," but "it is not good for man to be alone" (Gen. 2:18, Tobit 8:6). Marriage was very highly regarded among the rabbis. Only the Essenes (and only some of them) regarded continence as

---

[2] See J. Dupont, *Gnosis: la connaissance religieuse dans les épîtres de saint Paul* (Louvain, 1949); 327–77, esp. 371.

one of the highest ideals (cf. Pliny, *Hist. nat.* v. 17. 4 and other references in W. Bauer's article in Pauly-Wissowa, *Real-Encyclopädie der classischen Altertumswissenchaft* Suppl. IV 424). We may add that the Therapeutae also valued continence (Philo, *Vit. contempl.* 68). As Bauer observes, the common idea that the Essenes would not use wine or meat has no support in our sources for their views. They did, however, have common meals like the Christian agapé-eucharist. They also espoused a communistic way of life, and laid great emphasis on the concept of freedom. Some of them were especially skilled in prophecy (Josephus, *Bell.* ii. 159). They believed in the immortality of the soul rather than the resurrection of the body (Josephus, *Bell.* ii. 154; Hippolytus, *Ref.* ix. 27, is Christianizing, as Wendland notes).

Here we must admit that when we have said "the Essenes did or thought something specific," we cannot be absolutely sure that we are discussing facts. Bauer has pointed out the extent to which our sources reflect their authors' own theories and commonplace philosophical-ethnographical ideas of the time (*op. cit.*, 390–418). He concludes by saying that we cannot write a history of the Essenes. However, for our present purpose this consideration is irrelevant. We are dealing not with what the Essenes thought but with what others thought they thought. And it is obvious that for Philo, Josephus, and the Neoplatonist Porphyry (*De abstinentia* iv. 11–13) the Essenes represent the actual attainment of the ideal of the wise man. Philo's treatise *Quod omnis probus liber sit* (That every good man is free) is an interpretation of the Stoic wise-man-ideal and reaches its climax with the example of the Essenes. What they were thought to be was what influenced semi-philosophical minds.

In the ideal wise man as exemplified by the Essenes, then, we find the source of many of the problems within the Corinthian community. As the Essenes knew mysteries (Josephus, *Bell.* ii. 133) and had wisdom (ii. 158), so the Corinthians came to believe that they too were wise and free. The apostle's whole reply centers around the Christian idea of the grace of God. They have attained nothing; God has given them everything. "Why do you boast as if you had not received?" (I Cor. 4:7).

One more question may be raised. Since it was Paul who founded the church of Corinth, where did the Corinthians get their ideas of the ideal of wisdom? We may doubt (against W. L. Knox, *St. Paul and the Church of Jerusalem*, Cambridge, 1925, 313–14) whether Jewish partisans of Peter played much part in this situation. The conflict really seems to be between Paul and Apollos, or rather between adherents of each who misinterpret the views of both. Paul and Apollos are, or are made to appear, the principal antagonists (3:4–9). Apollos was a Jew of Alexandria, eloquent and well versed in the scriptures (Acts 18:24). His knowing "only the baptism of John" (Acts 18:25) might suggest that he understood John's baptism as Josephus did, as a ritual purification of the body (*Ant.* xviii. 117) like that of the Essenes (*Bell.* ii. 138). Paul's view of baptism is of course completely different.

We may suggest that it was Apollos who permitted the Corinthians to interpret their religion as a form of popular philosophy. Once the wise man ideal was introduced, it became possible to interpret it in two ways. One could follow the cynicizing Stoic ideal and stress the irrelevance of license. Some Corinthians seem to have followed this course. Alternatively, one could insist upon the importance of absolute continence with the later Stoa (cf. SVF III 563) and such groups as Essenes and Therapeutae. Both interpretations would stress the philosophical concept of freedom, itself introduced as an explanation of the apostle's rejection of the Jewish law. It is significant that Paul absolutely rejects the first interpretation while modifying and tempering the second. Possibly the latter interpretation is permitted not only because Paul himself is largely in agreement with it but also because it was set forth by his fellow worker Apollos.

Saint Peter's Epistle

by PHILIP CARRINGTON
Archbishop of Quebec

Two commentaries on I Peter have recently appeared in England, one by E. G. Selwyn, and the other by F. W. Beare. Both are fine works of scholarship; but one maintains the Petrine authorship while the other abandons it. Indeed, Dr. Beare is convinced that the case against it is overwhelming.

Dr. Selwyn does not, of course, suggest that the Apostle composed the Epistle personally or wrote it all out by hand without assistance; for the document itself forbids this hypothesis. It presents itself to the Church as an Epistle of Peter, but an Epistle written "through Silvanus"; and our first task is to discover what these words mean. Fortunately there are certain parallel instances which come to mind. There is the Epistle of the Church of Smyrna which relates the martyrdom of St. Polycarp, and is written "through Marcianus"; which cannot mean that Marcianus was simply the scribe or amanuensis, because the name of the amanuensis is given separately. Marcianus was the man who actually composed the letter. In the same way Dionysius of Corinth refers to the Epistle of Clement as an Epistle of the Roman Church "written through Clement"; Clement had composed it for the Roman Church. The same interpretation, in the absence of con-

trary evidence, may legitimately be applied to the case of I Peter;
written "through Silvanus" means that Silvanus composed it.

Dr. Beare, however, finds he cannot accept this interpretation;
he says:

> v. 12. διὰ Σ. ἔγραψα. . . . Silvanus is mentioned as the amanu-
> ensis, nothing less, but also nothing more. The employment of
> "ghosts" is not likely to have occurred to the Apostles, and the
> attempt to get round the linguistic impossibility of ascribing the
> letter to Peter by making Silvanus responsible for the good Greek
> is a device of desperation.

Would it be going too far to suggest that the tone of this passage
is a little too confident? And that the distinguished author has not,
perhaps, given sufficient attention to the strength of the case which
he describes as desperate? It seems to me, for one, that it is the text
of the Epistle itself, not the "device" of some desperate modern
scholar, that ascribes the good Greek to Silvanus; and if the word
"ghost" is a proper one to apply to the man whose name is put
forward in the document as its composer, why then the title will
have to go to Clement and to Marcianus as well.

In this passage Dr. Beare refers to the good Greek of the
Epistle as if that were his main argument against its authenticity;
but elsewhere he seems to prefer what he describes as "the clear
dependence on the Epistles of St. Paul"; a view of I Peter which
has become traditional in some schools of theology. It really does
not survive a critical comparison of the interesting parallels which
exist between I Peter, James, Colossians, and Ephesians. As the
reader of Dr. Selwyn's commentary can see for himself, the common material turns out to consist of liturgical or catechetical
phrases, or standard quotations from the Old Testament; and there
seems no reasonable doubt that these were derived by the writers
of these various Epistles, from baptismal catechisms, or other
sources, which were the common property of the Church.

The "clear dependence on the Epistles of St. Paul" vanishes

into thin air. All that can possibly remain is to ask whether the idea of writing an Epistle at all, and perhaps the general literary form which it took, may not have been suggested by the fact that Pauline Epistles in this form were already in circulation. One might go further and ask whether I Peter was not produced in the same scriptorium in Rome, by the same staff of book-producers which produced Ephesians. But this is mere conjecture.

Another line of argument against the authenticity of the Epistle is that which asserts that it cannot be dated so early as the Neronian persecution in 64, in connection with which (we are bound to agree) St. Peter died as a martyr. It is pointed out by Dr. Beare, in succession to numerous other scholars, that there is no other evidence to the effect that Christians in Pontus and Bithynia and adjoining provinces were at this time in danger of their lives because of persecution. The plain fact is that there is no further evidence, *period*; and the lack of evidence cannot be used to discredit I Peter. For all we know, Christians in Pontus may have been called upon to suffer "for the Name" *before* the great persecution in Rome took place.

Dr. Selwyn has pointed out that a sharp persecution had broken out in Judaea in 62 in which St. James the Just was martyred, "with others," as we know from Josephus; and Tacitus seems to link this Judaean persecution with the Neronian, by his reference to a second outbreak of Christianity "not only in Judaea, the birthplace of this evil thing, but even in Rome"; for in his mind a second outbreak would mean a second occasion on which the authorities were called upon to take cognizance of it.

The real objections to the authenticity of I Peter, in the mind of Dr. Beare and his school, are personal and theological. They arise from points of view which have become traditional now in certain quarters. The Epistle of St. Peter is not what such scholars would expect an apostolic writing to be like. It is in good Greek, it quotes the Septuagint, it indulges in occasional excellencies of style, it does not conform at all to their theories about Christian origins. Dr. Beare is surprised by the meagre references to the work of the Holy Spirit in the moral life of the believer; and yet St. Mark's Gospel, which is the companion piece to I Peter, is no different in this respect. He finds it hard to believe that an Apostle would describe the passion of our Lord in language drawn from Isaiah, and not in his own words; but perhaps the ancient familiar divine phrases, with their liturgical associations, meant more to St. Peter than Dr. Beare has allowed for. It all depends on the personal element; on sentiment, experience, and tradition.

Dr. Beare is deeply impressed with the mystery-religion theory of Perdelwitz, and builds up an elaborate case in his notes for the use of mystery-religion categories in I Peter. We would like to have seen him balance this interesting illustrative material with the more relevant material which may be drawn from Hebrew sources, including the Rabbinic. Was it necessary, for instance, to go as far as Zoroastrianism, to explain the metaphor of the gold in the furnace, when Ecclesiasticus 2:5 and Wisdom 3:6 were to hand? Dr. Beare admits on occasion that the Perdelwitz theory has its fragile spots, and that it reposes largely on evidence of a later date. It will probably turn out that we do not have to go beyond Hellenistic Judaism to explain the idiom of I Peter.

We must mention finally an all-embracing generalization to the effect that fictitious authorship was a "harmless literary device" often resorted to in the Jewish and Christian literature of the period. This opinion, too, fades into nothingness when confronted with actual facts; at least if taken in the sense in which Dr. Beare has received it. Everyone knows that a fictitious literature had arisen and was still in production among the Jews when I Peter was written; but all the books of this type were written in the names of ancient sages such as Solomon or Baruch or Ezra, who had flourished long centuries before. I have yet to come across any evidence to show that Christians or Jews were in the habit of exchanging letters which they signed with the names of contemporary persons, whether still living or recently dead. The time came, of course, when the apostolic literature had receded sufficiently far into the past to become endowed with a prestige of its own, and to be ranked as what we call classics; and when this happened, it became possible to produce a fictitious apostolic literature on the basis of these models. II Peter may be regarded as a perfect example of such a production; but all the arguments which go to prove the fictitious character of II Peter leave I Peter untouched; indeed, it may be said that they contribute, in reverse, to establish its authenticity.

The contrast is further emphasized by the fact that II Peter, looking back into the past, shows its acquaintance with an apostolic literature which was, by that time, classified as scripture; it included an Epistle of Peter which must be our I Peter.

In II Peter the stage is carefully set so as to re-create, in the imagination of the reader, a by-gone age; for a work of fiction is obliged to produce a complete illusion. In I Peter we have a few personal references of a casual character such as we naturally find in authentic documents. The fact is that I Peter bears no resemblance whatever to the admittedly fictitious literature of the Jews and Christians; and it is marked by an untheatrical sincerity and a profound gravity of utterance which are quite incompatible with artifice or with "harmless literary devices" of any sort. This is of course a personal judgment; but to personal judgments we must come at the end of our survey of the evidence. Our verdict is bound to be that we have been unable to find anything substantial in the case which has been put up against the Epistle; and those who accept it as authentic are following the evidence in the text and in the tradition of the Church.

APPENDED NOTE: The "simplicity" of I Peter does not exclude, of course, attention to literary form and accepted literary conventions; just as the "simplest" of poets may use metre and rhyme. Among these conventions are some of Semitic origin, which it has in common with Mark and with the Johannine books. The complicated structure of the Marcan Gospel is emphasized and held together by a system of "triads" or threefold repetitions, whether on a small scale within a paragraph or stanza, or on a large scale within the book as a whole. These will be set forth in a study of Mark which is now under preparation, to be called "The Primitive Christian Calendar."

The triads in I Peter are equally important; but they cannot be set out briefly, as various factors come into play, such as textual criticism, quotation from the LXX, and variation in the Greek word used. There is also the question of multiple triads; minor or local triads formed within major or extended triads. The following list, however, consists of words, occurring three times only, whether in close or extended range: *sojourners, Father, *consecration, obedience, bless, new-born or lately-born, hope, *resurrection, dead, *inheritance, etc., incorruptible, heaven, salvation, reveal, time (*kairos*), exult, revelation, to love (excluding a quotation from LXX), believe?, evangelize, be sober, faithful?, *love-of-brethren, hearts, into the age (excluding a quotation from LXX), guile (including such a quotation), *speaking-against, house or build-a-house, *be ashamed, disobey, people (*ethnos*), people (*laos*), conscience, *endure, unjustly?, shepherd, woman (wife), man (husband), righteous, *save, to think or be strange, love (the noun), elder, God (with grace).

This leaves, however, some interesting cases, in which the word occurs more than three times, and yet a triadic structure is observable, or can be suspected. The word "elect," for instance, occurs once in chapter 1; three times in chapter 2, forming a minor triad there; and again in chapter 5 in the compound form "co-elect," thus completing a major triad of three extended uses of the word. The word sufferings occurs once in 1:11, a second time in 4:13, and twice in chapter 5 (1 and 9); yet this is clearly a major triad consisting of three usages

* In these cases the Greek word is not identical: e.g., paroikia-paroikoi-parepidemoi, hagiasmos-hagiazein-hagnizein, anastasis-egeirein, kleronomia-sunkleronomoi, philadelphia-philadelphein-philadelphos, katalalein-katalalia, aischunesthai-kataischunesthai, hupopherein-hupomenein, sozein-diasozein, etc.

of the word in three extended passages. The following words are well worthy of study from this point of view: elect, grace, *unfading (taking in the word "withered"), faith, sufferings, time (*chronos*), *word (*logos* and *rhema*), flesh, *stone, will (of God), honour, sin, Spirit (and spirit).

Too numerous to be easily classified are the uses of: grace (including three minor triads), glory or glorify (three or four minor triads), holy (seven occurrences), call, conduct (seven occurrences), good and evil, good-doing and evil-doing, suffer (twelve occurrences: balanced perhaps by twelve occurrences of the word glory: the number which is symbolic of the holy people).

Geography and Climate in the Fourth Gospel

by SYDNEY TEMPLE
University of Massachusetts

When one travels about in Palestine during the winter months he is acutely aware of the relationship of geography and climate in the small area traversed by our Lord and His disciples in the gospel accounts. And when the traveller goes back to the Gospels to fit the unique conditions there prevailing with the Evangelist's accounts, he cannot help but be struck by the complete knowledge of the conditions in Palestine which is shown by the author of the Fourth Gospel. New light does seem to be shed upon the chronology of the life of Christ, at least as it was portrayed in that Gospel, when the geographical references in the text are considered in the light of prevailing local conditions.

1:28. Take, for example, the place of baptism "beyond the Jordan" for which there are sources to support both Bethabara (Authorized Version), Bethany (Revised Version, following Nestle), and Betharaba. The traditional place for the baptism is on the Jordan due east of Jericho, south of the present Allenby bridge. But one visit to that location will suggest the impracticability of that location for the purposes of John the Baptist, for in the winter the water there is deep and fast flowing between steep sand banks. The local Christian of the area will tell you that the place of baptism must have been much further north, above the Allenby bridge, where there are natural fords. In an aside he may tell you that these same fords are still used almost nightly for smuggling goods across the Jordan. The natural ford would be more practical for the purposes of baptism and would be a location where the preacher would be sure to find a ready audience. Geography suggests, therefore, that the place of baptism was at Bethabara, the ancient ford of the Jordan on the road to Gilead, which would be north of the present Allenby bridge.

The baptism must have taken place in the winter, for a popular preacher anxious to attract a crowd would take up that location only during the winter months. The exploratory excavations which were made by our party from the American School of Oriental Research this past winter have proved that Herod and his court moved to Jericho during the cold months, occupying the small city of villas which has been discovered at the place where the Wadi Kelt issues from the mountains. When the court moved to Jericho, all who could leave Jerusalem would follow, for it was there that trade was to be found and the warm winter climate attracted the crowds as well as the court. It would be in that area, then, that the Baptist would find crowds ready to hear his call to repentance and his message would not be unknown even in the halls of the palaces.

After April it became so unbearably hot in Jericho, which is 1,250 feet below sea level, that the recent excavation had to be stopped. There would be little point in anyone trying to carry on an evangelistic campaign in the lower Jordan valley after April. We are safe in assuming, therefore, that the baptism of Jesus took place at the Jordan fords in the winter months of the year.

1:43. Jesus journeys from the Jericho area to Galilee, and the conditions of climate tell us that he took the road along the Jordan River. During the winter months this is the natural and popular road, for it is level and pleasant. The upper road from Jerusalem to the north through the mountains of Ephraim can be very cold, as we know from bitter experience. After living in Jerusalem when there were about three feet of snow on the ground (approximately a meter) with no electricity to run oil furnaces and only kerosene pot-stoves in the cold stone buildings, we understand why Herod and Archelaus, with the respective courts, moved to Jericho in the winter.

2:1, 12. Following the Jordan valley north, Jesus and his disciples would have gone across the wide and today the wonderfully fertile Plain of Esdraelon, then mounted the hills to the north where Nazareth is situated. Kafr Kanna (Cana Village) lies deeper in the mountains on the road from Nazareth to Tiberias. From there they literally "went down to Capernaum," for the road from the hills drops sharply to Tiberias on the lake, then northward to Capernaum at the head of the lake. It is possible that the path missed Tiberias, cutting northward to the lake at Magdala, midway between Tiberias and Capernaum. In any event, the evangelist was correct in making no mention of a stop in Tiberias, for the Jews avoided settling in the city which Herod Antipas had built over an old cemetery.

2:13. Jesus literally went "up to Jerusalem," either traversing the Jordan valley and climbing the mountain trail up to Jerusalem from Jericho, or entering the mountains of Ephraim at Jenin and following the higher road south. The route he would take was probably determined by the date of the Passover that spring and, if one were curious enough, an astronomic compilation of the date of the Passover would probably tell the route that was taken on that particular trip.

2:22. The Master and his disciples remained in the high country of Judea after the Passover, baptizing in the manner of John. At that time the court had returned to Jerusalem and with it the crowds who had temporarily migrated to the winter capital. Jericho and the Jordan valley were now areas to be avoided, so the scene shifts to the cooler mountain district. John and his disciples were also located in the highlands at a well-known spring, Aenon, if Salim has been properly located in the hill country southeast of Shechem.

4:4. "He had to pass through Samaria," shows that the terrain and the season is being carefully followed in the account. Actually there is no necessity to pass through the heart of Samaria and by Jacob's Well, a short distance from Shechem, if it were the winter season and the Jordan road pleasant. But since summer was now approaching the Jordan route was unbearable, therefore the group going north would take the higher route, and so "had to pass through Samaria."

4:11, 20. The depth of the so-called Jacob's Well, is known to all travellers. The priest who lives at the Orthodox mission station there will let down a candle to show the depth of the water level, which is some 50 feet down in the wet winter season and as much as 85 feet below the ground-level toward the latter part of the dry season. To this day the women from the hill villages around are forced to come quite a distance to this well when the local water sources give out in the especially dry seasons (v. 15). The Samaritan Kohan in Nablus, where the new synagogue is situated on the western slope of Mount Gerizim, will still use the argument of the Woman of Samaria in contending that only on "this mountain" should the Passover sacrifice be held (v. 20). He can also prove to any who will listen that it was to this mountain that Elijah fled, seeking the counsel of Yahweh. The well is situated in the very shadow of the mountain, on the plain just to the northeast of its foot.

4:35. Following this order of seasons it is not difficult to place verse 35 in this place. The Passover and Feast of Massoth mark the early harvest, and the Day of First-Fruits, fifty days later, celebrates the second harvest. According to the time-schedule that is given in the gospel the grape harvest, the Feast of Booths, would be four months off. The reference to the fields as "white unto harvest" suggests a contrast of the wheat and barley festivals in the spring with the grape-gathering festivals in the autumn. Among the religious ceremonies which clustered at the general period of the autumn harvests was that of the Decision for the Year. Was Jesus contrasting the idea of waiting for a future decision with the very immediate prospect of reaping the harvest which was evident on all sides as the group walked through the valley? Though the simile takes some interpretation, the situation in regard to the crops and the time of the year certainly fits perfectly into the chronology of the account as given by the evangelist.

4:43. The group of disciples with their Lord proceed north through Jenin, drop down to the Plain of Esdraelon, climb past Nain and around Mt. Tabor, descending again to go along the Sea of Galilee to Capernaum.

5:1. Jesus goes up to Jerusalem again for a feast. It might be said that he returns for *the* feast, for in our Lord's day the celebration in the month of Tishri, the seventh month, was the primary festival of the year. From the exile the Hebrews had carried back with them a special emphasis on this festival which preceded the ancient celebration of the grape harvest, the Feast of Booths. The Babylonian New Year was begun with this fall festival during which the "ten terrible days of the world's judgment" set the fate of the nation for the year to come. That Assyrian custom was reflected in the fact that the Jews started the ecclesiastical year with Nisan, the Passover festival, but counted the civil year from Tishri. The festival began with the Day of Remembrance, marked by the blowing of trumpets on Tishri 1, developed to the Day of Atonement on the 10th of the month, and concluded with the Feast of Booths from the 15th to 21st. The prominence of this feast made it unnecessary for the evangelist to name it.

6:1, 4. The evangelist draws attention to the fact that the Sea of Galilee is also known as the Sea of Tiberias, so called for the city built in honor of Tiberius Caesar during the lifetime of our Lord. A winter has passed since the last reference to chronology, and the story picks up again six months later, at the Spring Equinox festival of the Passover. The cold winter winds have departed from the lake and in the spring sun the people sit down on the fresh young grass which has grown from the early and latter rains. It could not have been true that there was "much grass in the place" if the episode had been laid later in the summer, but in the short period following the rains small grass grows even in the "Wilderness of Judah" between Jericho and Jerusalem, and camels graze on the flat Jordan valley almost to the shores of the Dead Sea. The lake shores were covered with lush young grass at the Passover time, tempting the people to come out in the spring warmth to hear the young Preacher.

7:1, 14. Another half-year passes and this time reference is made directly to the Feast of Booths (Tabernacles), as distinct from the Days of Remembrance and Atonement. The statement, "Jesus went up to the temple and taught," raises an entirely different picture in one's mind after he has walked around in the immense temple area as it now exists, preserved and revered by the Mohammedans. Within the walled area there are two mosques and innumerable raised platforms for prayer groups. The area can only be compared to the parking lot around a football field to give the average Westerner an idea of its size and extent. At festivals the area must have been crowded with thousands of people, as it is today at Mohammedan feasts. Scattered throughout the area a hundred different prophets and teachers could expound their doctrines and dispute with one another, and each find a large and ready audience. Jesus' teaching in the temple must be thought of in this way, as a sort of ecclesiastical Hyde Park corner on Empire Day.

8:1. The doubtful section contained in the first eleven verses of chapter eight continues to give a picture of the area which fits well into the details of the terrain. Jesus and his disciples would quite naturally camp on the "Mount of Olives," the slope across from the west wall of the city which to this day is covered by an olive grove except for the part taken up by the several churches of Gethsemane. At the pilgrimage feasts in Israel thousands gathered, camping on the hillsides about the city. The present St. Stephen's gate, which leads from Gethsemane, enters the city wall just north of the temple area, while the so-called Golden Gate (now closed) entered directly into the temple close which forms the southwest corner of the walled city of Jerusalem. Because of its convenience to the temple, the Mount of Olives must have been covered with the temporary dwellings of the pilgrims at the great feasts of the Jewish year.

10:22. "It was winter and Jesus was walking in the temple, in the portico of Solomon." The picture of our Lord walking under the covered porch brings memories of winter precipitation to any who have spent that season in Jerusalem. While a meter of snow is unusual, there is normally some snow during the winter because of the altitude of Jerusalem, about 1800 feet above sea level. But winter in the hill country of Palestine is memorable for the rains. Truly the heavens seem to open as the tumult of the winter rains comes; one is reminded of the story of Noah's ark, for it is easy to believe that forty days of such rain could inundate the whole land. The Feast of the Dedication, the Hannukkah, which celebrated the freeing of the Holy City by the Maccabees, comes just in the season of the former rains, in the twelfth month, Chisleu. The mention of the portico shows that the author knew the seasonal vicissitudes of the Palestinian climate.

10:40. After the Feast of Dedication the "social season" opened at Jericho. The court and all who were not forced to remain in Jerusalem for business reasons would move to the Jordan valley, for January and February are the cold months. In going from Jerusalem (1800 feet above sea level) to Jericho (1250 feet below sea level) one travels twenty miles horizontally and the better part of a mile vertically. During January we could often pass through some thirty degrees of temperature morning and evening as we went from 40° in Jerusalem to 70° at Jericho, and reversed the process in the evening.

11:17, 18. Bethany is, of course, on the main road from Jericho to Jerusalem. The road climbs constantly from the Jordan valley to Bethany, then, turning a corner past Bethany, one sees the whole of the walled city laid out before him. The town is not called Bethany in Arabic today but "The Village of Lazarus."

11:54. Though the winter is severe for a people living in stone houses with insufficient heat, it passes quickly. By early March the grass has started to grow on every barren hill, and soon the countryside becomes red with the anemones which look much like our "Flanders poppies." There are also to be found, on all sides, the "lilies of the field" (Matt. 6:28), a lovely white lily, rather thick-petaled, with the blossoms from six to twelve inches from the ground. We saw these from the ruins of ancient Shiloh to Petra, south of the Dead Sea. It is in this setting that the author places Jesus and his disciples in that last short period between the breaking of spring and the final Passover. He concludes the travels of the disciples and their Master at Bethany, just over the Mount of Olives, as they come for the preparatory days of the festival week preceding the Passover (12:1).

This equating of local conditions with the description of events in the Fourth Gospel is not intended as an argument for any particular place of origin or authorship for the work. It does show, I believe, that the author of the original draft, before it was worked over by redactors, did have an intimate knowledge of conditions in Palestine. If he did not gain this knowledge from direct or indirect acquaintance with the actual events in the life of Jesus, he was at the very least a careful workman who made his chronicle fit the geographical and climatic details of the locale of his story.

Soma Christou

by CLARENCE T. CRAIG
Drew University

Few phrases in the New Testament carry as profound theological significance as that of "the body of Christ." At the same time, there is wide difference of opinion concerning its historical origin and even greater divergence regarding its religious implications. The newer understanding of the anthropology of Paul and the possibility of influence from Gnostic Urmensch and aion speculation have called for the re-examination of the doctrinal formulae in these areas.

I assume that there is no need to differentiate between the full phrase "body of Christ" and "his body" or "my body," or simply "the body" where the context identifies the body as his. There are gospel passages where the dead body of Jesus is called *soma*,[1] but these fall outside our discussion. Elsewhere, the term is applied in three ways which appear to be entirely different: (a) the physical organism which was crucified on Golgotha; (b) the bread which was broken in the upper room and at each succeeding celebration of the Lord's Supper; (c) the Church which had been redeemed by Christ.

[1] Mark 15:43; Matt. 27:58-9; Luke 23:55; 24:3, 23; John 19:31, 38, 40; 20:12. Acts 9:40 is an additional example.

I

As long as Greek anthropological assumptions governed Christian thought, this variety of applications was not too disturbing. From the Greek point of view, the body was not constitutive of the person. It was an instrument or organ to be used by the soul or the mind.[2] Modern idealistic thought took for granted the same psychological dualism. The person or soul has been looked upon as immaterial and this might express itself through various material media. Thus it was not difficult to hold that the one Spirit of Christ was present to men in these three different ways.

But Hebrew anthropology was quite different. Here there was no thought of a soul imprisoned in a body. The body was the total person as viewed from one point of view. The various parts of the individual were simply forms of appearance of the one living person. The evil impulse was not located in the body in contrast to the mind,[3] but infected the whole person. To use the oft-quoted words of J. Pedersen, "The body is the soul in its outward form." [4]

There is no longer real dispute at this point. The crucial question concerns the nature of Paul's anthropology, for it is in his writings that the meaning of the body of Christ raises the most difficult problems. Lüdemann,[5] Holtzmann,[6] and many other nineteenth-century interpreters were confident that Paul's view of man was determined by a Hellenistic dualism. Body, flesh, and the outer man were set over opposed to mind, spirit, and the inner man. The one essential Christ, therefore, possessed three different kinds of body.

This understanding of Paul's anthropology has not only been

[2] Ernst Käsemann, *Leib und Leib Christi,* Tübingen, 1933, pp. 23–59.
[3] Strack-Billerbeck, *Kommentar zum N. T. aus Talmud und Midrasch,* IV, pp. 480 ff.
[4] Joh. Pedersen, *Israel,* I, London, 1926, pp. 170 f.
[5] Herm. Lüdemann, *Die Anthropologie des Apostels Paulus,* 1872.
[6] H. J. Holtzmann, *Neutestamentliche Theologie,* II, 2 ed. 1910, p. 291.

challenged; I should say that it has been completely demolished. The careful investigation by Gutbrod has shown that Paul's usage is essentially Hebraic.[7] Käsemann had supported the same conclusion in his *Leib und Leib Christi* and this result is elaborated in Bultmann's New Testament Theology.[8] In I Cor. 15:35 ff. there does seem to be influence from the Greek point of view. "With what body do they come" assumes that some distinction is drawn between the person and the body. But in the main Paul looked upon the body as the person. When he says that "sin should not reign in our mortal bodies"[9] but we should present our "bodies to God as a living sacrifice,"[10] he was not referring to the physical organism but to the person as a whole.

Once this view is accepted—and for its substantiation I must refer to the monographs mentioned—we see that the earlier studies on the "body of Christ" have become in large part obsolete.[11] The apostle was not referring to the body which *belonged* to Christ but to the body which *was* Christ. This faces us with the searching problem of how Christ could be three apparently different things. It is not that he *has* three bodies; there are three ways in which he *is* a body, and difficulties arise in regard to them all.

II

We shall begin with the references to the actual physical body of Christ. Reconciliation has come in the body of flesh by his death;[12] man has died to the law through the body of Christ[13] in his vicarious, representative death. Post-Pauline interpreters con-

[7] Walter Gutbrod, *Die Paulinische Anthropologie*, Stuttgart, 1934.
[8] Rudolf Bultmann, *Theologie des Neuen Testaments*, Tübingen, 1948, pp. 188 ff.
[9] Rom. 7:12.   [10] Rom. 12:1.
[11] Traugott Schmidt, *Der Leib Christi*, Leipzig, 1919. Also in part A. Wikenhauser, *Die Kirche als der Mystische Leib Christi nach dem Apostel Paulus*, Münster, 1940.
[12] Col. 1:22.   [13] Rom. 7:4.

tinued to join redemption to the body or person. "He himself bore
our sins in his body on the tree." [14] In the words of the author to
the Hebrews, "We have been consecrated through the offering of
the body of Jesus Christ once for all." [15] In all of these passages
soma is used essentially in the Hebraic sense and denotes the sacrificial giving of the person in the work of salvation. But in contrast
to some early Christians, Paul insisted that the resurrection body
was not the same as the one which had been laid away. Yet surely
the crucified and risen Christ was one and the same person. Some
modification in a unitary conception of body is introduced at this
point.

In the Communion passages ambiguity seems to be possible
because in the Aramaic language no verb would have been used to
express the exact relationship between the bread and the body.
Conceivably Jesus may have intended "represents" rather than
"is." But both Mark and Paul wrote *estin*.[16] This too is not without ambiguity, for the apostle could also say that Christ *was* the
rock.[17] Such midrashic interpretations, however, are hardly comparable to the situation presented in the eucharist. Whether the
emphasis lay on the *breaking* of the bread or upon its *distribution*,
in either case it is the *person* of Christ who is given for the many.

The bread is related not to a physical organ used by Christ's
spirit, but to Christ himself. "This is my body" meant "This is
myself."

With the Church as the body of Christ we are dealing with a
terminology which is confined to Paul; this was his unique contribution to ecclesiology. To some degree it was anticipated in the
Synoptic Gospels in the long list of sayings where disciples are
identified with Christ: "He who receives you receives me"; [18] "As
you did it to one of the least of these my brethren you did it to

---

[14] I Pet. 2:24.   [15] Heb. 10:10.
[16] Mark 14:22; I Cor. 11:24.   [17] I Cor. 10:4.
[18] Matt. 10:40.

me." [19] But that does not go beyond the identification of the king with his subjects. The author of the Fourth Gospel may have had the figure in mind when he interpreted the saying of Jesus about raising up this temple in three days as referring to his body.[20] With typical Johannine double meaning this may refer to the Church as well as to his resurrection body. Only Paul and the author of Ephesians, however, specifically refer to the Church as the body of Christ. We are not dealing with a New Testament conception but with a peculiarly Pauline one. In contrast to the other two usages, Paul's terminology was not necessarily an inherited one, but may have been formed in relation to his own anthropology.

The concept of the Church as the body of Christ should not be isolated from the equally characteristic Pauline formulae, "in Christ" and "Christ in you." Deissmann's [21] mistake did not lie in interpreting these in a primarily local sense or in describing this relation to Christ as "mystical." His failure lay in the insufficient stress upon the new eschatological situation and on the incorporation of the believer into Christ's own body. Bultmann [22] and the Barthians are just as one-sided in their attempt to exclude all mysticism from Paul. On this point the "consequent eschatology" of Schweitzer is more balanced even though he was unduly hostile to the admission of any Hellenistic influence.[23] Believers were baptized into the one body of Christ, and so were in him and he in them.[24] The Messiah and his people comprised one corporeity. The Church is the body of Christ because it has been taken up into him, that is, into his body. We shall trace the development of this expression in his letters.

[19] Matt. 25:40.   [20] John 2:21.
[21] A. Deissmann, *Die Neutestamentliche Formel "in Christo Jesu,"* 1892.
[22] R. Bultmann, *op. cit.*, p. 307. A strong opponent of the mystical interpretation is E. Lohmeyer, *Grundlagen Paulinischer Theologie*, Tübingen, 1929, pp. 139 ff.
[23] A. Schweitzer, *The Mysticism of the Apostle Paul*, New York, 1931.
[24] I Cor. 12:13.

III

I Corinthians is the earliest extant letter to contain this conviction. It does not appear, however, as philosophical speculation but is applied in connection with practical exhortations to the community. (a) The congregation was in danger of being split into factions. But this would mean nothing less than dividing up Christ himself, for the Church was his body.[25] (b) Again, to be joined to a prostitute would involve nothing less than uniting a member of Christ's own body in this way. Since that is impossible, such sexual sin separates one completely from the body of Christ.[26] (c) Finally, the variety of functions of the members of a human organism provide the analogy for the variety of gifts within the Church.[27] These gifts are the work of the Spirit, but this fact should not obscure Paul's conception of the nature of the body. Both here and in Rom. 12:5 Paul was thinking in terms of the varied parts of the one organism. Variety in unity is not the only truth involved, but it is an important aspect of the identification of the community with the body of Christ.

Likewise in Colossians the oneness of the body to which they were called is related to the need for peace and harmony in the community.[28] Because Christ dwells *in* Paul, the sufferings which he undergoes complete what remains of Christ's afflictions for the sake of his body.[29] The organistic aspect is not stressed as much as in I Corinthians, yet it is clearly implicit. Though Paul was himself part of the body, his activity is spoken of as on behalf of the body. Nevertheless, there is unquestionably a new emphasis in Colossians, and that is the relation of the body to its head.[30] As such, Christ is the source of growth for the organism,[31] which through him is knit together into one whole.

[25] I Cor. 1:13.
[26] I Cor. 6:15.
[27] I Cor. 12:14–27.
[28] Col. 3:15.
[29] Col. 1:24.
[30] Col. 1:18.
[31] Col. 2:19.

Many interpreters find a sharp contrast here to the presentation in I Cor. 12. There, the head is simply one of the more valuable members of the body; here the head has absolute preeminence. These interpreters assume that the rest of the body is a rump attached to the head. But that understanding assumes that Paul is using *kephale* in Col. 1:18 in the same way that he did in I Cor. 12:21. In I Cor. 11:5, however, the "head" is not used anatomically but refers to the person to whom obedience is due. I believe that in Colossians Paul introduces the new idea of Christ as the "head" in connection with his insistence that all of the divine *pleroma* dwelt in Christ. Those "in Christ" should not give service to the elemental spirits, for believers receive all from the one who is not only the head of the church but also of every rule and authority.[32] As the first-born from the dead, he exercises authority over the whole body.

IV

This emphasis in Colossians is repeated in Ephesians. There is one body [33] of which we are members [34] and Christ is the head.[35] In this letter the mention of the husband as the head of the wife gives strong support to the conclusion that "head" is not used with anatomical reference. In still other ways Ephesians carries on the genuinely Pauline point of view. The various ministries, elaborated even beyond those enumerated in I Corinthians 12, are for building up the body of Christ.[36] Likewise, as in Col. 2:19, he is the source of bodily growth through his function as the "head." [37] At the same time, the Church appears as a quite separate entity which needs to be consecrated and cleansed by a Savior.[38] But in

[32] Col. 2:10; 1:18.
[34] Ephes. 5:30.
[36] Ephes. 4:12.
[38] Ephes. 5:26.

[33] Ephes. 4:4.
[35] Ephes. 1:22; 5:23.
[37] Ephes. 4:16.

the very same context, the author insists that the love of Christ for the Church is a love for his own body.[39]

In two directions, however, Ephesians introduces differing points of view. These lead me to draw the line between genuine and non-genuine at this point rather than with Colossians. First, the author extends the concept of the Church as the new Temple by identifying the foundation as composed of apostles and prophets.[40] The second development involves the relationship of the body to the head. This is complicated by the fact that the verse in question [41] is capable of varied interpretations. If the word *pleroma* is taken in apposition with Christ, there is no contrast with Colossians. But it is highly unlikely that the author separated so far words which he intended to go together. Commentators divide on whether *pleroumenou* is middle or passive; but whether Christ is the one filled, or the one who fills, it is still the Church which is the *pleroma*. Paul wrote in Colossians that all the divine *pleroma* dwelt in Christ. Here in Ephesians the idea is that the Church is necessary to make Christ complete. To use the words of Mersch,[42] "the whole Christ" is Christ and the Church. Christ is incomplete without the Church, as his body the Church is inseparable from the totality of his person. .

V

Thus far we have ignored three important passages where the classification is disputed. How are we to understand Eph. 2:16, that "he might reconcile us both [Jew and Gentile] to God in one body through the cross"? The parallel in Col. 1:22 is clear because

[39] Ephes. 5:29–30.   [40] Ephes. 2:20.
[41] Ephes. 1:23.
[42] Emile Mersch, *The Whole Christ*, London, 1938, tr. by John R. Kelly. A vigorous defense of a literal instead of a figurative interpretation as the author traces "the historical development of the doctrine of the Mystical Body in Scripture and Tradition."

there we read the "body of flesh," the historical person and act on Golgotha. But here in Ephesians is not the "one body" the Church? Dibelius [43] has so contended, and sees here one of the important terminological distinctions between Colossians and Ephesians. While the cross refers to the historical ground of the reconciliation, the one body is the Church, within which all distinctions have been abolished. I think that this interpretation is correct, though the distinction in the very nature of the case is not absolute; Christ and his Church comprise one body together and are united in a single corporeity.

The second disputed passage is I Cor. 10:16. In what way is the bread which believers break a "participation in the body of Christ"? The parallel with the cup leads most interpreters to assume that it is the so-called eucharistic body of Christ. On the other hand, in the following verse Paul speaks of the "many who are one body." Kümmel [44] argues that this expression concerning the unity of the Church determines the emphasis throughout the entire paragraph. Participation in Christ's blood is participation in the benefits of his redemptive death. Participation in the body of Christ is union in his Church, a relationship strengthened in and by the Lord's Supper. Personally I find it more plausible to hold that the reference is to the eucharistic food. Paul's conclusion is not that the participant in idol worship cannot be a member of two cult communities; rather, he cannot belong to two lords.

The third passage is I Cor. 11:29, where Paul says that a failure to discern the body will bring judgment on the participant. Does this mean a failure to discern the connection between Christ and

[43] M. Dibelius, in *An die Kolosser, Epheser* (*Handbuch zum N. T.*, 2 ed., Tübingen, 1927).

[44] W. G. Kümmel, in *Handbuch zum Neuen Testament, An die Korinther*, von Hans Lietzmann, 4th edition, Tübingen, 1949, p. 182. In citing Ernst Käsemann, "Anliegen und Eigenart der Paulinischen Abendmahlslehre," *Evangelische Theologie*, 1948, pp. 264 ff., Kümmel does not make clear that Käsemann does not support him at this point.

the bread? Or is it a failure to discern that the Church itself is Christ's body and therefore must not be filled with division and disorder? Moffatt,[45] Kümmel,[46] and others think that Paul had in mind the Church. I cannot see that this is the primary reference. Unworthy participation through gluttony, drunkenness, and un-brotherly haste hardly arises from a lack of discernment of the unity of the body, but from a failure in love toward the breth-ren.

But must we draw a sharp line between the three senses in which the "body" is used? Nowhere does Paul say that Christ is a Trinity with three bodies. They are different aspects or manifesta-tions of the one Christ. Frequently Christians speak of the "mysti-cal body" of Christ, but there is not the slightest New Testament support for such a phrase. Nor do we find any such term as the "eucharistic body" of Christ. The New Testament knows only the body of Christ; the very unity implied in the word forbids our thinking of three different entities. Decision concerning the exact balance of reference in these three passages is difficult just because of the fluidity of the concept.

VI

Even greater difference of opinion is found concerning the in-fluence which led Paul to refer to the Church as the body of Christ. Some find sufficient explanation in the understanding of the Lord's Supper. The community of believers which here *par-takes* of the body of Christ thereby *becomes* his body.[47] Others go out from the organistic application and find its origin in the Stoic figure of the state as a body which is found in contemporary

[45] James Moffatt, *The First Epistle of Paul to the Corinthians*, London, 1938, pp. 171 ff.
[46] W. G. Kümmel, *op. cit.*, p. 186.
[47] A. E. J. Rawlinson, "Corpus Christi" in *Mysterium Christi*, edited by G. K. A. Bell and A. Deissmann, London, 1930.

Hellenistic writers.[48] Appeal has also been made to the Gnostic aion speculation in which the redeemer is the head of a gigantic body which comprises the new man resulting from the incorporation of the redeemed into the redeemer. Schlier [49] and Käsemann [50] elaborated the Reitzenstein [51] theses in this direction without being more bound than the noted philologist by strict attention to chronological relationships. Though Scandinavian Protestants have been quite negative in their reaction to the theory,[52] Roman Catholic investigators have been more impressed with the strength of this influence.[53]

Personally I am suspicious of a genealogy which is constituted either by appeals to avowedly later documents or to sources far removed from the writing to be explained. In any case, Paul and his pupil should be interpreted not in terms of the supposed source of their borrowing but from their own exposition. In these writings, the Church appears not only as the body of Christ but as an entity composed of members who still retain very much of the "old man." Though the individual should have died when he was baptized into Christ, he still needed the warning to put away all "anger, wrath, malice, slander, and foul talk." [54] The various members are not "Christs" even though they may be said to have been incorporated into his body.

Though Paul's reference to the Church as the body of Christ

[48] W. L. Knox, "Parallels to the N. T. use of *soma,*" *Journal of Theological Studies,* XXXIX (1938), pp. 243-46. S. Hanson, *The Unity of the Church,* Uppsala, 1946, p. 52.

[49] Heinrich Schlier, *Christus und die Kirche in Epheserbrief,* Tübingen, 1930, pp. 37-48.

[50] Ernst Käsemann, *Leib und Leib Christi,* Tübingen, 1933, pp. 59-94.

[51] Richard Reitzenstein, *Das Iranische Erlösungsmysterium,* Bonn, 1921.

[52] Ernst Percy, *Der Leib Christi,* Lund, 1942; pp. 39 f. Stig Hanson, *The Unity of the Church,* Uppsala, 1946, pp. 113 ff.

[53] A. Wikenhauser, *op. cit.,* pp. 232-40. A much more reserved attitude is taken by L. Cerfaux, *La Théologie de l'Eglise suivant Saint Paul,* Paris, 1948, 2 ed., pp. 281 ff. It is quite rejected by Werner Goossens in *L'Eglise Corps du Christ,* Paris, 1949.

[54] Col. 3 :8.

is more than a metaphor, it must not be isolated from all of the rest
which he has to say about the Church. It is not possible to find
complete consistency of presentation. Though aion speculation
may have had some influence on Paul, modifying to a degree the
original eschatological framework of his message, that reconstruc-
tion was not complete. The messianic community is described
from a new point of view, but the old perspective is not entirely
left behind. In any case, the Church has not become a pre-existent,
Platonic idea.[55] It is still the corporate result of the historic act of
God's redemption in Christ. It is one way of expressing the indis-
soluble union of the people of God with the agent of deliverance.

VII

In closing, three observations should be made which bear upon
the theological evaluation of the evidence. First the identification
of the Church with the body of Christ is found in only one segment of the New Testament tradition. It is but one of the ways of
expressing the relationship between Christ and the people of God.
To make this normative would be to absolutize the part rather
than the whole. Neither in the later books of the New Testament
nor among the early fathers for whom Paul was authoritative was
this conception the sole line of development.

Whenever special emphasis is laid upon this interpretation (and
I wish to be included among those who find it both illuminating
and helpful) one distinction which is often made is logically ex-
cluded. Some say today that though members of different denomi-
nations are one in Christ they do not all belong to the one Church
of God, for certain essential qualifications of the Church are lacking. This contention may be possible as long as the Church is
defined in other terms. But if it *is* the body of Christ, this claim
is impossible. We have seen that the body is not an external instru-

[55] Cerfaux finds the primary source of what he calls the celestial church in
the heavenly Jerusalem in Judaism and her personification in the virgin bride.

ment which the person uses on occasion. For Paul, the body is the person. To be in Christ and to be in the body of Christ cannot be different. Contrariwise, if an individual is not in the body he is not in Christ.

Finally, the conception carries with it difficulties in relation to the doctrine of the Trinity which are not usually recognized. Complications arise at once when Christ is regarded no longer as that particular *aion* through whom the worlds were both created and redeemed but as the second person of the Godhead. Are believers part of the body of God? Are they taken up into Deity and made one with Him, not in terms simply of the union of spirits but of a single corporeity? Views of that type run athwart the empirical evidence. The difficulties presented indicate why this conception will always elude fully consistent exposition. But the figure does express better than any other how indispensable the believer is to Christ and that his very life depends on union with the Lord. Some would rather express this truth through such a figure as that of a vine and its branches,[56] but the body is closer to the level of the life with which religion is concerned. With all its difficulties, *soma Christou* will always remain one of the most valued descriptions of the true nature of the Church.

[56] John 15:1–10.

Preaching from the New Testament: An Open Letter to Preachers

by MORTON S. ENSLIN
Crozer Theological Seminary

Real preaching from the New Testament is a desperately exacting task. It requires a lot of knowledge to which there is no easy road. But it is a tremendously rewarding task which, when properly done, pays rich dividends to both the congregation and the preacher himself.

You will note I said "real preaching from the New Testament." The fact that a sermon is prefaced by a text from the New Testament, mentions frequently the name of Jesus, is tinctured with a diction of mildly archaic flavor, and is thus presumably (or hopefully) biblical, does not make it preaching from the New Testament. Preaching from the New Testament, at least as I understand the term, is of the sort which reveals the nature and quality of the New Testament—what it is, and, equally important, what it is not—not preaching of a sort which evidences the cleverness of the preacher in discovering a phrase, which can be twisted or perverted, to seem to buttress with divine support his own quite different notions.

It has long been the habit to quote the word of the Psalmist, when trying to describe the Bible: "Thy word is a lamp unto my

87

feet, and a light unto my path." It could be and should; too frequently it is not. Instead it has often been a distinct handicap and
liability—and largely because of the failure of us preachers. So long
and so often we have referred to it as God's word, as being in a
peculiar and altogether unique sense the revelation of God, complete and entire, that many people have come to regard this as
literally the case. Thus a woman recently wrote me: "We must
not be broader than God's law. And anything which He did not
command us to teach [not, mark you, "nothing which He commanded us not to teach"] should not be embraced by His people
and incorporated into His church." For her, God's law was set
forth in its completeness in the Bible. For two thousand years God
has been silent. And do not delude yourselves: there are thousands
of people in America—many of them in your churches—who
believe precisely that today. That was the view of orthodox Judaism at the time of the beginning of Christianity; it was the view
of the daughter religion. Everything which seemed to be under
the blessing of God—and which they approved—was believed to
have been foreseen by God and included in his all-embracing revelation. Thus a premium was put on ingenuity in finding by allegorical interpretation the new in the old.

Some of these interpretations and findings which have accumu-
lated through the years seem so crude and bizarre that we easily
dismiss them or make jokes about them. There was the case of
the frontier Baptist preacher named Waterbrooks who visited a
city church and saw a baptism. The costume of the minister, especially the rubber trousers, intrigued him. On his return home he
sought the support of his deacons for this important advance, only
to be met with the crushing rejoinder: "It is not in the Bible." But
when he read them the opening words of Psalm 42, "pants for the
water brooks," he received their unanimous support. I do not
vouch for the story, which I have known from my boyhood; I do
insist it is no more arbitrary or unwarranted than the attempt

through the centuries to find Jesus plainly foretold in the pages of Holy Writ; that found the gentile mission written in invisible ink in the pages of the Old Testament; that found one incident after another in the life of Jesus foreshadowed centuries before; that found his birth from a virgin and God in the divine word to the serpent: "And I will put enmity between thy seed and *her* seed; he shall bruise thy head, and thou shalt bruise his heel"; that discovered further proof of this same biological miracle in the unfortunate mistranslation into Greek of the words of Isaiah: "Behold a young woman is with child, and is about to bear a son"; or discovered support for the story of the flight into Egypt from the words of Hosea, "Out of Egypt have I called my son."

And once the writings we call the New Testament had acquired the dignity of age and had aroused the devotion and love of Christians through years of familiarity and repetition, they too, in turn, were found to be equally replete with all the answers to life's developing queries. I have long known an orthodox denomination which bitterly opposes the use of tobacco but which is quite placid toward the use of intoxicating liquors. And their position is, they are convinced, strictly biblical. None less than Jesus himself had expressed himself with finality on the subject. Had he not said, "Whatsoever thing from without entereth into the man, it cannot defile him . . . that which cometh out of the man, that defileth the man"?

It would not be difficult to multiply these examples. And it would have its value, for the cumulative weight would scarcely fail to make all but the most obtuse aware of this peril. And peril it is. It is this notion of the Bible, which has been fostered through the years, which has so utterly obscured its real values. In the eyes of many it has become a magical repository of all wisdom, all truth, an all-inclusive encyclopaedia of religion and ethics, providing short-cut and ready-made answers to all of life's enigmas; in the eyes of many others it is a tiresome, archaic book which preachers are supposed to like to read and from which they can prove anything, but for which intelligent people have little time and less interest.

Frankly, I do not know which of these estimates is the more deadly. Of one thing I am sure: both are vicious, and both are unnecessary. If preachers would awake to the real challenge that confronts them, that it is vastly more important to encourage their people to be interested in the Bible—yes, I will sharpen that word, to *love* the Bible—than it is to try to make them believe it, a good many traffic signals along life's highways would turn from red to green.

How many in your congregations know the story of the New Testament, know why it was that so many years went by before any of the twenty-seven books, which they are now supposed to prize, were written; why it was that the gospels were among the last of the books to be framed; why there are so many amazing agreements between the gospels—especially between three of them —and at the same time such flat and irreconcilable contradictions? How many in your congregations know why Paul wrote his letters to those churches in Corinth, in Philippi, in Thessalonica, in Galatia; know that he had no thought of writing Holy Scripture, but was simply trying to aid them in straightening out some problems which had arisen, in no small part, because they had failed to understand what he had preached to them when he had been with them; that he was writing *to them* and not (over their heads) to subsequent ages of Christians; that neither Paul nor the one he was preaching as Lord had dreamed there ever would be "subsequent ages" which would need or be interested to know? How many in your congregations know that there were many other gospels, letters, apocalypses, written in those early years and which, in many cases, were for centuries as highly regarded as— some for decades at least more highly than—some of those which we now have? How many of them know why it was that eventually these which we now prize came to be regarded first as worthy to be read with the "real Scriptures" (the Old Testament), then to be of equal value with the older writings, and finally to surpass them? How many in your congregations know that for centuries there was wide and heated difference of opinion as to what was, what was not, Scripture? How many, that between the earliest of these twenty-seven writings and the latest a full century elapsed and that in that time many views and beliefs, many hopes and dreams, had radically changed; that an additional two hundred years elapsed before the earliest copies of these writings which we now possess were penned, and that in these many decades of copying thousands of differences, accidental and deliberate, came to be included; that today we have many thousand early copies of the New Testament in Greek, Latin, Syriac, Coptic, and other languages into which they were translated, and that no two of them are in identical agreement; that at a conservative estimate 150,000 variant readings occur?

Have you in your ministries, in some cases extending over many years, sought to make materials of this nature clear to your people? Have you sought to let them see that in the New Testament they have a library of many books, written by many men of very different minds; that these men had not infrequently to depend for their information on what we call sources, some written, some oral, and that they felt perfectly free to revamp, to reinterpret, the material in the light of the day in which they lived? Or have you encouraged—by commission or omission—your congregation to gather the impression that actually God wrote the New Testament; that he chose various individuals, to be sure, to do the actual work, but that he guided their fingers so that they were, so to speak, writing more wisely than they knew; that a Mark or a John (I use the traditional names of these two evangelists for convenience, not from conviction) were supernaturally guided as they wrote about Jesus in a manner different from Xenophon and Plato when they wrote about Socrates?

Have you put your congregations in a position to consider with their minds such a word as "Judge not that ye be not judged" in view of the blistering woes and accusations against the Scribes and Pharisees which Matthew reports were uttered by the same man; to ponder the word of Matthew to the Twelve, "Go not into any way of the gentiles, and enter not into any city of the Samaritans," with that of Luke (regarding these same men), "and he sent messengers before his face, and they went, and entered into a city of the Samaritans, to make ready for him"; to reflect upon the word at the end of Mark from the angel to the women at the tomb to tell the disciples to go to Galilee, that it was there that they should see him, together with such stories as Matthew gives of the final parting of Jesus from his disciples and his Great Commission to them from a mountain top in Galilee, and the haunting story of his appearance on the shores of Galilee's lake with his thrice-repeated searching question to Peter—to reflect upon these stories in the light of the seemingly utterly contradictory account in Luke and Acts that Jesus had expressly ordered his disciples to remain in Jerusalem, that it was there that they should receive the Holy Spirit, and their obedient waiting and its reception at Pentecost? What help, if any, have you given them when, after they have read the story of Pentecost with its vivid account of how the disciples received the promised Spirit, they chance to read (or hear read) in the Gospel of John that on the night of the Easter Sunday Jesus had appeared to his disciples, had breathed on them and said, "Receive you the Holy Spirit"?

Or do you feel that these matters are irrelevant, that in the hands of experts perhaps they are proper, but that they would be of a nature, if generally known among laymen, to undermine confidence in the Bible? Frankly, gentlemen, this appears to me a

fundamental question. Do you believe in the New Testament, do
you prize it for what it is, or have you substituted for it a carefully
expurgated and rewritten version? Be honest with yourselves.
Suppose this situation: one of your members who has read the
New Testament asks you, either privately, or more embarrassing,
in a public meeting, when you have just drawn some material from
one of these examples, how you reconcile it with its exact opposite,
also in God's Holy Word. Just what will your answer be? Are
you in a position to answer it intelligently and honestly? Will you
be ready so to do, or will you sidestep it with an unctuous and
heart-warming glow on your face (but with great uncertainty and
pain in your brain) that in God's great mine many jewels are to be
found, not all alike, but each of value and useful in its own proper
place? Or will you try to avoid it with a wisecrack or implied re-
proof, and then say to yourself, when that other member in the
audience, whose face lights up at the question and seems so eager
for your reply, slips quietly away and is not so regular at subsequent meetings, that it is sad to see the depressing inroads of the
secular, that people are not so eager to come to church as they
once were? There are many times when we find ourselves, with
no warning at all, in an extraordinarily accurate pair of scales and
in the process of being weighed. And to change the figure, in
many of these cases, the postman does not ring twice.

At the beginning of this letter, I said that real preaching from
the New Testament was an exacting task, that it required a lot of
knowledge, and that there was no easy road. I repeat it. Too often
I hear preachers say easily, and at times, as it seems to me, a bit
too self-satisfiedly: "I accept the findings of modern scholarship."
Fine as far as it goes; but too often it does not go anywhere at all.
To preach effectively from the New Testament, to make these
writings live and glow for your people, to encourage them to love
and read them, to see them for what they are and to prize them,
not to regard them as a sort of magical set of answers to life's

demands, a ready reckoner which will fall open at the appropriate
place if approached after the appropriate word of incantation—
this requires a deal more than a general and vague feeling that
scholarship and research have probably turned up a lot of valuable
stuff regarding the New Testament; that on the whole higher
critics are not such terribly destructive people—except a few who
have, of course, gone beyond the bounds of all decency—that probably, after all, the stuff you had had to wade through in New
Testament introduction back in the Seminary could be used in
preaching after it was buffed up a bit, and that you will have to
have a look at it some of these times when you can get around to it.

This all too common attitude may, to be sure, lead the preacher
to refrain from doing what some of his colleagues are doing, who
loudly announce on every and no occasion that they "believe the
Bible from cover to cover," namely, giving a positive and constant
course of indoctrination, the net result of which is the perversion
of what should be a lamp to the feet into a lamp-post from which
to hang all their brethren who do not agree with them in their
interpretation (or misinterpretation) of the book which they so
loudly quote and lustily thwack. But it does very little toward
providing the positive picture which seems to me so largely
lacking.

"Accepting the findings of modern scholarship" is not enough.
To make effective use of the New Testament, a preacher must be
at home in it, must know not only what is in it but what is not,
must be at home in the first century, must himself be familiar with
the story of how we got the New Testament. The thesis of education at this point, at least as it was dispensed to me, that the "skills"
and "methods" are the essential thing, which translated into terms
of this particular problem would seem to be, "To preach effectively
from the New Testament you must learn a few more tricks of
pulpit legerdemain," appears to me nonsense. I once knew a
woman who had taught German for years in high school, and I

was led to believe that she had done it very effectively—was, in fact, a natural as a teacher. When later I learned that when she went to Germany she had to find a shop where English was spoken before she could purchase a pair of gloves, I became a bit skeptical as to how valuable her teaching through the years had been. Skills and methods may be very fine, but they cannot take the place of content. Before a man can teach effectively, can make his subject live and glow, he must know his subject. And this is as true of the New Testament as it is of German.

The theological seminary was the place to get your start for such an equipment, but it is only a start. It must be kept up and used. It is only as we seek to teach others that we really learn ourselves. If through the years you have kept growing, have not laid aside your notes and sold your books; if you keep ever before your eyes the task of showing to your people riches that are becoming increasingly valuable to you, you can do it, and effectively. You can lead any congregation, once it has come to have confidence in you as a friend and brother, to welcome you in times of joy and sadness—you can lead any congregation to appreciate and approve values which you manifestly have found yourself.

For a man to be in a pulpit for five years and to say of findings of scholarship, "I agree with this, but I can't present it to my people, for they are not ready for it," is to convict himself of utter incompetence. There is no subject which a minister cannot discuss frankly and honestly with his people after he and they have summered and wintered one another through the years. Gradually, quietly, winsomely he can—and he will if he genuinely holds and prizes views as truth—present them over the years, lead his people step by step until there are no closed doors between pulpit and pew. And a congregation like that will be utterly freed from the possibility of being stampeded or led on a rampage, come what may.

The trouble is largely with ourselves. We preachers have been derelict. Too frequently we have refused to pay the price of leadership. This course which I have been trying to sketch out requires work, gruelling work. The people are ready and eager for it. To the average man and woman outside the church—and if we are honest, we will admit that the average man and woman are outside the church—the Bible is a book that preachers talk about, that contains a lot of ridiculous stories about the world being created in six days, of city walls falling down when men shouted, of floating ax-heads and talking donkeys, of whales swallowing men, and of bread and fish being multiplied by a word of incantation. They don't believe these stories—and I for one do not blame them—for all the facts of life seem to demonstrate the opposite. That is what the church stands for, they believe, and quite rightly they are not having any. When they hear religious broadcasts, they hear nothing to disabuse their minds as to what Christianity is—at least insofar as it has to do with the Bible. The fundamentalists on every occasion whoop up precisely this note; the occasional preacher of more solid and wholesome approach, who has more recently been gaining access to the air, does not discuss these matters at all. He does not wish to be controversial. It is below his dignity. He may do a fine job, but he does nothing to correct this widespread notion.

There is a solution, will we but take it. It is not one of appeasement. I have no pleasure in chip-on-the-shoulder preaching. Ridiculing notions, however absurd they may seem, which are dear to people, is always of doubtful propriety. But that does not mean that we must acquiesce. Ridicule, sneering, innuendo, raising a laugh—they are inexcusably rude; but a positive, appreciative, broadgauged presentation is a very effective weapon, especially when it is in the hands of a man you admire and trust. But while it will not try to do everything in one sermon, may be content to keep battering slowly and remorselessly, aware that centuries of ignorance may take years, not hours, of correction, it will be constantly on its guard never to backtrack. What it says, it will say clearly and un-mistakably. It will not call white black in order to get poor old Widow Jones to put it on. The old widow may have had a new lease on life and have decided that she has been in mourning long enough. And even if she still intends to remain loyal to the memory of the late-lamented, she may be properly annoyed at you for trifling with her affections and doubly so at your thinking that she is color-blind. Say what you have to say so that people know what you mean. If you are not ready to have people understand you, keep your mouth shut.

I am not advocating that a preacher consider himself a lecturer on New Testament criticism and that he try to give his congregation a course in archaeology, source analysis, and textual criticism in ten easy lessons. Even farther from my mind is the desire that he seek to retail over his pulpit some critical theories which in the seminary he dutifully transcribed into his notebook without in the slightest degree having seen their cogency, simply because this seems startling and will prove him a keen-eyed and square-jawed liberal, or some suggestion which he has picked up at a lecture he attended and promptly appropriated as his own without it having made the slightest dent on his own mind. That is simply cheap and vulgar publicity stuff. It is because of such occasional antics that many congregations have become skeptical of higher criticism. Short-cut methods like those are farthest from my mind. But I am convinced that any preacher of reasonable intelligence, who has had a respectable training, can, without turning himself into a third-rate lecturer or his pulpit into a classroom desk, present winsomely the foundation materials for a sane, wholesome, and essentially sound attitude toward the New Testament and its world.

The ministry was once a learned profession, a company of scholars. That this situation, and not its reverse, is the ideal would seem to me indisputable. Too frequently the scholar has been burlesqued as one remote from life and chronically dull and dry-asdust. It is time to utter a ringing protest at this utterly unwarranted contention. There is no earthly reason for scholarship, either in or out of the pulpit, to be either dull or remote. When that is the case, it is simply due to faulty craftsmanship. Accuracy and exactness and fidelity to facts can be made to appear pedantic and unattractive, but this is utterly unnecessary. And there is no better place for the preachers of our day and generation to start out in a quiet way toward refuting that utterly unwarrantable misconception than in what should be their joy as well as obligation: presenting the New Testament in the only way worthy of its origin and treasures.

Miracles and Adamnan's Life of St. Columba

by A. HAIRE FORSTER
Evanston, Illinois

It is probable that most of the articles for Dr. Grant's *Festschrift* will be in the field in which he is himself so eminent, and although this one is outside that field it is on a subject which has some bearing on the New Testament.

Adamnan was born twenty-seven years after the death of St. Columba and therefore in his youth had the opportunity of getting information from old men who had known the Saint. Furthermore he was, like St. Columba, a Donegal man and eventually became Abbot of Iona; thus his life was spent in places where local traditions about his famous predecessor would be preserved. It is surprising and for us rather disappointing to find that his book is not a biography at all but a collection of prophecies, miracles, and visions. The last chapter on the death of St. Columba shows that he could write biography in the modern sense and do it with simple and engaging charm.

St. Columba was a contemporary of the Emperor Justinian, and died in the year that Gregory the Great sent St. Augustine to England. He was of royal blood both on his father's and his mother's side, and had he not become a monk he might have been King of Ireland—a first cousin of his did in fact become High King of Ireland. His appearance was imposing, his voice musical and of unusual range, his temper quick, at times violent. This last characteristic Adamnan is inclined to tone down, yet even he writes "de adversariorum terrificis ultionibus." In addition to the name Columba, a dove, he had a second name Crimthain, a wolf. His anger, it should be said, was usually aroused by acts of cruelty and injustice, particularly to the poor and weak. Kindness to animals was one of the rules at Iona, and there are many stories which illustrate this side of his character; for instance, how his white pony shed tears into his breast as he sat weary by the wayside on the day of his death, and how he gave his blessing to the animal as they parted. Under his rule, Iona became famous for hospitality and, if visitors arrived on a fast day, the fast was relaxed. As might be expected from his ancestry, St. Columba was a statesman and took part in the politics of his time: he might be listed among the makers of Scotland. In his day Ireland was known as Scotia or Hibernia; Adamnan uses both names in the same chapter. A colony of Scotti from northeast Ireland had settled in Dalriada, the modern Argyle. North of this colony was the Kingdom of the Picts under King Brude. These Picts, who were heathen, had attacked and defeated the Scotti of Dalriada in 560. St. Columba sailed to Iona in 563. His plan was to convert the Picts and so promote harmony between them and his countrymen in Dalriada. He had already had contacts with Picts in Ireland; his foster father was Cruithnechan, a Donegal priest, and his name would indicate a Pict. What is now County Down was inhabited by Picts. Two of these were friends of the Saint, St. Comgall and St. Cainnech, and he prudently took these with him when he made his daring expedition to the palace of King Brude, situated near the modern Inverness. King Brude was won over to his side and though perhaps never baptized supported his mission. Dalriada at this time paid tribute to the King of Ireland, but St. Columba later on obtained "Home Rule" and freedom from tribute for the colony at the synod of Drumceatt in northern Ireland. He was accompanied on that occasion by Aidan, King of Dalriada, whom he himself had ordained as king. This Aidan was not the next heir to the throne, but St. Columba, according to the story, was instructed in a dream to ordain him and the people agreed—a remarkable example of the Saint's prestige.

He was a poet as well as a statesman, and in his youth studied with a Christian bard called Gemman, from whom it is said he learned Latin. Adamnan unfortunately gives no specimens of his poetry nor indeed does he give any example of his preaching. Several undoubtedly ancient poems are attributed to him but none of them can be proved to be genuine. One of these old poems, which might be his, is called *A Prayer for Travelling*, and contains two verses which would serve as a motto for preachers:

> Life be in my speech,
> Sense in what I say.

Part of the agenda at the Synod of Drumceatt was to abolish the Order of Bards whose insolence and exactions had become intolerable. St. Columba spoke for them and they were allowed to continue with reduced retinues and the requirement that they should live more by their own labor and less by other men's generosity.

So much for St. Columba as a missionary, a statesman, and a poet. The fact is that these activities are only incidental, almost accidental, in Adamnan's book. Adamnan's real interest is in his prophecies, miracles, and visions. The book was written at the request of the monks of Iona, and the mind of the age *required* miracles by a saint; they were no difficulty, they were a necessity. The Life would be read aloud to the assembled monks, and if it contained no miracles it would be like a love story with no love scenes. Then again in Ireland, and more so in his mission to the Picts of Scotland, St. Columba was in frequent conflict with the Druids—called Magi by Adamnan. These medicine men worked

wonders by the aid of demons, in the opinion of the monks; a
Christian saint must work bigger and better ones. Adamnan's
St. Columba is in many respects unintelligible to us; he was intelligible to his own age. Some of these marvellous tales Adamnan
got from an earlier book, *De virtutibus Columbae*, written by a
former Abbot of Iona, Cuimine; Adamnan's third book seems to
be largely a reproduction of Cuimine. Others he got from men
who had been eye witnesses, or who had heard them from eye
witnesses. Adamnan no doubt accepted them all as he received
them; it is impossible for us to do so. Some are inventions based on
Bible miracles, as when Columba, as a deacon, turned water into
wine when the wine could not be found at a celebration of the
Eucharist; others are exaggerations of real events. As Aristotle said
in the *Poetics*, "Now the wonderful pleases; of which this is an
indication, that all men when they want to gratify their hearers
add something to what they relate."

Thus it was told how he sailed down Loch Ness against a
strong wind raised by Druid magic. Now Columba must have
been a skillful boatman—he had to be, among the tides and currents
and storms of the Scottish islands. If the tide were running in, a
boat might move against a contrary wind. I have seen a boat in full
sail with a following wind move backwards in trying to get up
Strangford Lough; the tide had turned and was running out.
St. Columba knew the tides and also the weather signs and could
often "prophesy" storm or calm or change of wind. He was said
to have moved the flow of a river in order to let the salmon get up
to spawn, but a "Life" compiled by O'Donnell in 1532 makes him
move the stones which blocked the water. It is just possible, too,
that some of the Saint's own poetic fancies were translated into
actual incidents by his ardent disciples, as the poem about the sun
standing still becomes a fact in Joshua 10:12–14.

Yet when we have finished explaining the wonders as the
results of natural causes or as exaggerations or inventions or as

dreams turned into visions or poetic phrases made into actual incidents, there is a remainder which need not be so accounted for.
When new ideas are received without distrust from an impression
of authority, and expectancy is thereby stimulated, cures do result;
they are usually called cures by *suggestion*. Now St. Columba was
just the man to work such cures: he came from a race of kings, and
kings were supposed to have the gift of healing. Even Charles II
of England was believed to have the magic touch. St. Columba's
reputation as a saint and a scholar was spread far and wide, his
benedictions or maledictions would be expected to succeed, and
it would seem that they often did. What is known about Psychotherapy and Suggestion throws some light on the inscrutable, that
which the writers of the sixth century called the "miraculous" in
St. Columba's life. He himself would have explained it quite simply
as due to the power of God brought into action by his fervent
prayers along with the prayers of his monks or companions.

Psychotherapy helps to make more intelligible to us some of
the miracles of St. Columba, but he was said to have even stranger
gifts than that of healing. Adamnan's Life gives many stories of
his "Second Sight." Those who believe in telepathy and clairvoyance are often dismissed as psychological racketeers; scornful
phrases, however, do not decide a question. In Browning's poem,
Sludge the Medium, Sludge says:

> This trade of mine, I don't know, can't be sure,
> But there was something in it, tricks and all.

An unprejudiced person cannot read *Telepathy and Clairvoyance*
by Dr. Tischner, a volume of the "International Library of
Psychology, Philosophy and Scientific Method," or the seventh
volume of *Proceedings* of the (British) Society for Psychical
Research, without at least suspecting that there is "something in
it." A position between credulity and contempt is required by
some of the facts presented. Dr. Tischner in his Introduction says

that most of the experiments reported in his book were made in the presence of a medical commission, called into existence after a lecture which he gave before the Medical Society in Munich. Here are two of the testimonies of observers. From Dr. Schede: "The experiments I witnessed with Miss von B. in 1913 have led me to conclude that it was a case of genuine clairvoyance, as trickery and other modes of deception were made impossible by the arrangement of the experiments." From Professor Gruber: "As experiments in which the object was known to no living person were positive, I take it that clairvoyance is definitely proved, telepathy being impossible under the circumstances." In the seventh volume of the *Proceedings* of the Society for Psychical Research, a case is reported of clairvoyance—and of clairaudience as well—in which the son of Bishop Lee of Iowa saw and heard in a dream his father, who was several hundred miles away, fall downstairs. The incident is related by the son and agrees exactly with the accident as reported by Bishop Lee to the Bishop of Algoma. This is one of several similar cases recorded in an article by Mrs. Henry Sidgwick, "On the Evidence for Clairvoyance." Just as the range of temperatures of thermometers is only a small segment of the temperatures in existence, so it would seem that there are supernormal faculties of the mind possessed by some, and if we assume that St. Columba was endowed with these, his prophecies and visions, though distorted and exaggerated by his disciples, are not altogether impossible.

When asked to explain his "Second Sight," St. Columba replied by what might now be called a theory of Cosmic Consciousness. "Some there are," he said, "though very few, to whom divine grace has granted this: that they can clearly and most distinctly see at one and the same moment, as though under one ray of the sun, even the entire circuit of the whole world with its surroundings of ocean and sky, the inmost part of their mind being marvellously enlarged." According to the stories, he used his gift to good purpose. It is often related that when he became aware that a friend was in danger from sickness or enemies or was in peril on the sea, he would summon his monks to the chapel and pray for the one in need and would know when the prayer was answered. His mediumistic powers were not used for gain or display, but in the service of his beloved communities.

There are two prophecies of St. Columba which make a fitting conclusion to this essay. More than once he foretold the time of his death. Those who now are beginning to study Parapsychology would call this *Precognition*. Swedenborg did the same, as related in a letter to John Wesley. The other prophecy was uttered on the last day of the Saint's life as he stood on the hill above the monastery at Iona: "Upon this place, small though it be and mean, not only the kings of the Scotic people with their peoples, but also the rulers of barbarous and foreign races with the people subject to them, shall confer great and no common honour."

NOTE. The name Iona is a scribal error. The island was called Hy or I, and Adamnan makes from this the adjective Ioua and calls the place the Ioua Insula. The u as often happens in manuscripts was confused with n, hence Iona. Since Iona can represent the Hebrew for Columba (dove) the mistake held its ground.

The Descent of Jesus in Muhammadan Eschatology

by ARTHUR JEFFERY
Columbia University

Though the doctrine of the Second Advent of our Lord may not hold a very important place in the theology of the New Testament, it was a doctrine that caught the imagination of the Eastern Churches in the non-Greek-speaking areas of early Christendom, and through the teaching of those churches it has come to have an important place in the Muslim accounts of the Last Things.

Like other teachings, taken over by Muḥammad and his followers from the earlier religions, this has had its own peculiar Muslim development, but it is a development which is of sufficient interest to be brought to the attention of a wider audience than that of the handful of specialists in Muslim theology.

Whether Muḥammad himself taught a doctrine of the Second Coming of Jesus is somewhat uncertain, though the consensus of later Islam is that he did. There are two passages in the Qur'ān which are generally taken to be references to this event. Both are in Madinan passages from the later years of Muḥammad's ministry. The earlier is in XLIII, 61:

Verily he is knowledge [1] of the Hour, so be not in doubt about it, but follow me.

Since it is Jesus who is being spoken of in the verses which immediately precede and succeed v. 61, this is usually interpreted to be a reference to him and so the pronoun is translated "he." There are, however, those who translate "it," and take the reference to be not to Jesus but to the Qur'ān. The second passage is in IV, 159/157:

There are none of the People of the Book but will assuredly believe on him before his death, and on the Day of Resurrection he will be a witness for them.

Here it is argued that since many obviously did not believe on him while he was on earth the reference must be to his second coming at the end of time, when he will be the agent of the great conversion of all men to the true faith. Some Muslim commentators see a third reference to his Second Coming in III, 46/41:

He will speak to the people in the cradle, and as a grown man, (and will be) one of the upright,

where the word used for "grown man" is *kahl*, but according to Muslim belief Jesus was taken up to heaven when he was still at that age when a man is known as a *shābb*, so that while it is true that he was one of the four infants who spoke in the cradle,[2] he did not speak to men as a *kahl* at his first coming, so the reference must be to his speaking to them at his second coming. Some see a fourth reference in XIX, 33/34; where Jesus says:

---

[1] This follows the *textus receptus* which reads *'ilm*, "knowledge," but there is a variant reading *'alam*, "sign" or "mark," which would support the later Muslim theory that the Second Advent of Jesus is one of the signs of the arrival of the Hour.

[2] That Jesus spoke in the cradle is mentioned also in Sūras, V, 110/109; XIX, 30/31. The three others were (i) the son of Pharaoh's daughter, i.e. Moses; (ii) the child who was a witness to the chastity of Joseph; (iii) the companion of Juraij. See at-Tabarī, *Annales,* I, 383.

"And peace is upon me the day of my birth, and the day
of my death, and the day of my being raised alive,"

for according to IV, 158/157 (cf. V, 117) Jesus did not die on the
cross but was snatched up to Allah, while his likeness was cast on
another who was crucified in his stead, so his reference to his dying
and being raised alive can only be to events connected with his
second coming.

When we turn to the *Ḥadīth*, those collections which embody
the Traditions concerning the sayings and doing of Muḥammad
which, next to the Qur'ān, are normative for the belief and practice
of Muslims, we find that in the earliest stratum of this *Ḥadīth*
material the only references to a Second Coming of Jesus are those
which refer to his "descent" to do battle with *ad-Dajjāl*, the Anti-
Christ. Thus we read:

He will descend at the moment of their worst distress
under the great famine,[3] for a voice will call from heaven to
men: "Rejoice! succor comes." Then Jesus will descend and
will rejoice with them as they rejoice. They will say: "O
Spirit of Allah,[4] lead prayers," but he will say: "Allah has
given the honour to this community (i.e., the Muslims), so no
one ought to lead them [in prayer] save one of themselves."
So their *Amīr*[5] will lead them in prayer, and Jesus will pray

[3] The famine is one of the forms of distress brought by the Anti-Christ:
"When he is here there will be three terrible years, in one of which the
sky will withhold one third of its moisture and the earth one third of its
verdure; in the second the sky will withhold two thirds of its moisture and
the earth two thirds of its verdure; in the third the sky will withhold all its
moisture and the earth all its verdure, so that there will remain no animal that
has not perished. This will be the worst trial of ad-Dajjāl."
'Alī al-Qārī, *Mirqāt*, V, 212, 212; Aḥmad b. Ḥanbal, *Musnad*, VI, 125, 455;
Nuwairī, *Nihāyat al-Arib*, XIV, 284.

[4] In Muslim writings Jesus is often referred to as "Spirit of Allah" because
in Sūra IV, 171/169 he is spoken of as "a spirit from Him," i.e., from Allah.

[5] *Amīr* means "leader," "chief," but in later forms of the Tradition it is
said that this was not just the prayer-leader who was in charge locally at that
particular moment, but was the Mahdī, and that Jesus prayed behind him to
show that he was now a Muslim belonging to Muḥammad's community of the
faithful. See Pseudo-Balkhī, *Kitāb al-Bad'*, II, 191, 192.

behind him. When it is ended Jesus will call for his spear and go after ad-Dajjāl.[6] He will say: "Go gently, O Dajjāl, O lying one." When ad-Dajjāl sees Jesus and recognizes his voice, he will melt away like lead in a fire, or like suet in the sun, and had not Jesus said: "Go gently" to that melting, there would have been nothing of him left. Then Jesus will leap at him with his spear, stab him between the breasts and kill him.[7] Then he will scatter his hosts (i.e., the hosts of ad-Dajjāl's followers) among the stones and trees. The majority of his host will be Jews and Hypocrites, so the stones will cry out: "O Spirit of Allah! here is an unbeliever behind me, so kill him!" [8]

Some such story of a connection between the descent of Jesus and the slaying of ad-Dajjāl must have been in circulation very early in Islamic history, for there was an Arabic proverb, "When the Messiah kills the Messiah" (*Lisān al-'Arab*, III, 430), which can only be explained as a reference to the day when the Messiah Jesus on his second advent will kill the false Messiah ad-Dajjāl, i.e., when the true Messiah kills the false one.

In later groups of Tradition we find the "descent" of Jesus appearing in other connections. One such group connects it with the Millennium:

> Said the Apostle of Allah: All the Prophets are brethren, the children of one family though of different mothers, and their religion is one and the same. I am next in succession to Jesus son of Mary, since between him and me there has been no Prophet. So when ye see him give him recognition. He will be a man of middle height, reddish-white in complexion, wearing two turmeric-coloured tunics, i.e., garments dyed yellow,

---

[6] The full title of the Anti-Christ is *al-Masīḥ ad-Dajjāl*, which is, of course, the Syriac *msīḥā daggālā*—ψευδόχριστος. He is also sometimes called *al-kadhdhāb*, "the confirmed liar," which explains the "O lying one" in the *ḥadīth*, and sometimes is referred to as *al-Masīḥ aḍ-ḍallāl*, "the Messiah who leads astray."

[7] It will be remembered that the notion of the Messiah killing his enemies with his own hand is found in II Baruch, XL, 1–2; LXXII, 2. It doubtless derives from the more ancient idea of the Messiah as warrior.

[8] *Kanz al-'Ummāl*, VII, No. 2939.

and his head will be perfumed though unmoistened. He will break crosses and kill swine and make wealth abound. (Quoted by ash-Sha'rānī in *at-Tadhkira*, p. 133. See *Kanz*, VI, No. 1963; VII, No. 2142.)

The longer form of this Tradition has the Prophet say:

"Jesus will be over my community as a just judge and an upright *Imām* [i.e., leader]. He will break crosses and kill swine. He will suppress the *jizya* [poll-tax] but leave the *sadaqa* [alms-giving]. No sheep or camel will be attacked, all disputing and hating will disappear, the poison of all poisonous things will be removed, so that a male child may put its hand into a serpent's mouth and not be harmed, and a female child handle a lion without its hurting her. A wolf will be among the flocks as though it were their sheep-dog, and the earth will be filled with peace as a water-bottle is with water. There will be but one word [i.e., all men will be in agreement], and no one will be worshipped save Allah. War will put up its weapons, the Quraish [9] will be deprived of their rule, and the earth will be as though of silver, producing its verdure as it did in the days of Adam." [10]

In a still later form of this *ḥadīth* we read:

Jesus, said the Prophet, will descend among you and will be my Caliph to govern you. Let any one of you who lives long enough to see this give him my salutation. He will kill swine and break crosses, and will make the pilgrimage to Mecca at the head of 70,000 pilgrims, among whom will be the Seven Sleepers [11] who will fulfil the pilgrimage rites. He will carry an Azdite [12] woman. Hate, enmity, mutual rivalry

[9] The Quraish were the "merchant aristocracy" who ruled Mecca in the days before Islam, and who captured the Caliphate again in the Umayyad Dynasty, much to the disgust of the "old Muslims."

[10] Tirmidhī, *Ṣaḥīḥ*, XXXI, 54; Aḥmad b.Ḥanbal, *Musnad*, II, 406; Nuwairī, *Nihāya*, XIV, 283.

[11] Their story, as Muḥammad could remember it, is told in Sūra, XVIII.

[12] The Azd were one of the most widely ramified tribal groups among those said to have come up from South Arabia, and in the troubles between the tribes in the Umayyad period it was they who stood out as champions of the southern Arabs.

will disappear from the earth, which will again be like it was in the time of Adam, so that a camel fattened in summer can be left alone and no one will touch her. Then you will see sheep with wolves, and little children playing with serpents which will not harm them. In his days Allah will spread justice in the earth so that the mouse will no longer gnaw at the leather sacks, and a man will be summoned to receive money but will not take it. In that day a single pomegranate will suffice for a household.[13]

Another group of Traditions associates his "descent" with the "Remnant," and the coming of the hosts of Gog and Magog. A fairly early *ḥadīth* had reported the Prophet as saying:

> "Jesus will descend to eight hundred men and four hundred women who are the choicest of all on earth in those days, as though they were the goodly ones of those who have departed." [14]

These are the "Remnant" who remained faithful in spite of the deceits and persecutions of the Anti-Christ, and are those to whom Muḥammad referred in the *ḥadīth*:

> There will always remain a band of my community who fight for the truth, and come forth openly before the people, caring not who may be against them, till Jesus comes.[15]

The coming to them of Jesus is that he may shelter them from the ravages of the hosts of Gog and Magog:

> There will come to Jesus a community [or in some texts— Jesus will come to a community] whom Allah has preserved from ad-Dajjāl, whose faces he will anoint, and whom he will tell of the degrees of bliss they will have in Paradise. While he is doing this Allah will say to him: "Lo! I have brought forth servants of Mine against whom no one is able to fight, so preserve My servants at aṭ-Ṭūr." [16]

[13] Ibn al-Wardī, *Kharīda*, p. 281; Pseudo-Balkhī, II, 190, 191.
[14] *Kanz*, VII, No. 2149; ash-Shaʿrānī, *Tadhkira*, p. 133.
[15] *Kanz*, VII, Nos. 3012, 3013.
[16] ʿAlī al-Qārī, *Mirqāt*, V, 198; *Kanz*, VII, No. 2026.

These servants of Allah whom none can resist are the hosts of Gog and Magog, and the place aṭ-Ṭūr, to which Jesus takes the faithful remnant to keep them safe, is said by some to be Mt. Sinai, but by others, with more likelihood, to be the Mount of Olives. Their distress during the days of the ravaging of the hosts of Gog and Magog will be so great—

> that the head of a bullock [i.e., the least succulent part] will be more precious to them than a hundred dīnārs are to a man now (*Mishkāt al-Maṣābīḥ*, p. 474).

So at their request Jesus will pray to Allah and a swarm of gnats will be sent to destroy these barbarian hordes.

> Then Jesus and his companions will set themselves to prayer, and Allah will send against the hosts gnats which will enter into their necks, so that they will perish like the dying of a single soul. Then Jesus and his companions will come down into the land, but will not be able to find a spot as big as a span which is not filled with the fetid smell of them and their foul stench. So Jesus and his companions will pray and Allah will send birds who in size are as the necks of Bactrian camels, who will take them and cast them away wheresoever Allah wills. Then Allah will send a rain which will miss neither house nor hair tent, and which will wash the earth so as to leave it like a mirror. Then the earth will be told to produce its fruits and get back to its blessedness.[17]

In the schematizations worked out by the later writers on eschatology these various forms of Tradition concerning the Descent of Jesus are brought under the section dealing with the "Signs of the Coming of the Hour." That there would be certain signs indicating to men that the Hour was drawing near had been already indicated in the Qur'ān, where in Sūra XLVII, 18/20 we read:

> So do they expect anything other than that the Hour should come suddenly upon them. The conditions for it have

[17] Ibn Makhlūf, *al-'Ulūm al-Fākhira*, I, 128, 129.

already come,[18] and when it comes upon them whence will they get their warning?

Also in a very early Tradition we are told about a man coming to the Prophet and asking when the Hour would arrive, to whom the Prophet replied that about that matter the questioned was no better informed than the questioner. So the man asked were there any signs by which one might take warning of its nearness, and the Prophet answered:

> "When you see the slave-girl giving birth to her mistress; when you see the shoeless fellow, the naked, the destitute, and uncouth shepherds (or herdsmen) building arrogantly high houses, then it is near." [19]

At first there was no suggestion of any particular number or order among these signs, but in the later schematizations they were arranged and there were said to be seven "lesser signs" and seven "greater signs" which heralded the approach of the Last Day. These "greater signs" are those which interest us. They are:

    i. The arrival of the Mahdī.
   ii. The appearance of the Beast.
  iii. The coming of ad-Dajjāl, the Anti-Christ.
   iv. The Descent of Jesus.
    v. The arrival of Gog and Magog with their hosts.
   vi. The rising of the sun from the West, causing a great upset.
  vii. The destruction of the Ka'ba at Mecca by the Abyssinians.

[18] That is, the signs of its coming are already showing. That Muḥammad himself expected the imminent arrival of the Hour is suggested by the *ḥadīth* already quoted in which he asks those of his followers who are there when Jesus arrives to convey to Jesus his greeting. Paul Casanova in his book, *Mohammed et la fin du monde* (Paris, 1911), has gathered together a lot of curious evidence which suggests that Muḥammad expected the Last Day in his own lifetime.

[19] Muslim-Nawawī, I, 158; *Kanz*, VII, Nos. 1667, 1668, 1816, 1830. Various fanciful interpretations of this *ḥadīth* have been suggested, but the sense of it is that a sure sign of the approaching end is when you see such an upheaval of social life that those normally regarded as on the lowest rungs have come to be those on the highest rungs of the social ladder.

Four of these are intimately connected with the Second Advent of Jesus.

A. *The Mahdī*

The Mahdī, whose figure has been so fateful in Islamic history, even down to comparatively modern times, is in a sense a *Muhammedus redivivus*.[20] The word *mahdī* means "the rightly guided one," and could be, and indeed has been, used of various historical personages,[21] but in the eschatological treatises it is the name of a future deliverer who will appear in the Last Days, coming from the East, to restore the fortunes of Islam.[22] The Prophet is reported to have said:

"When the world has only a century to live Allah will send a man of my family, who will fill the earth with justice as it has been filled with injustice, whose name will accord with mine, and whose father's name is the same as my father's name,"[23]

a tradition which is sometimes expanded to read:

He will make oppression disappear from the earth, will spread justice, establish equity between the weak and the strong, spread Islam from the East to the West, and leave no one on earth who does not either accept Islam or pay the poll-tax.[24]

This Mahdī idea may go back to a very ancient conception of a returning king which had continued alive in the popular thought

[20] See in particular Casanova's book mentioned above, p. 53.

[21] Examples are given by Goldziher, *Vorlesungen*, pp. 363 ff.

[22] It is noticeable that in some of the Traditions there is nothing properly eschatological about him, he is merely a dreamed-of deliverer who will come to rescue the Muslim community from some distressful situation which has no relation whatever to the Last Times. In most Traditions, however, he is a figure in the eschatological drama.

[23] *Kanz*, VII, No. 1931; 'Alī al-Qārī, V, 179; Pseudo-Balkhī, II, 181.

[24] Pseudo-Balkhī, II, 182; Ibn al-Wardī, p. 279.

of the people of Muḥammad's day as it continued alive in Western Europe.[25] It was an idea well rooted in the Old Testament,[26] which in later Judaism developed in connection with the figures of Enoch, Moses, and Elijah.[27] The expected Tāheb of the Samaritans is a Moses redivivus.[28] Among the Zoroastrians the expectation of the coming Saoshyant is an expectation of a second advent of Zoroaster,[29] and the Mandaeans teach that after the reign of a false Messiah there will be a return, before the End, of Anūsh 'Uthrā.[30] It is thus not impossible that in Muslim popular thought there grew up independently a belief in some sort of second advent of Muḥammad before the coming of the End. The fact, however, that no such eschatological figure as the Mahdī is to be found in any of the early collections of *Ḥadīth*, nor in the earliest Creeds, nor in the writings of any of the early theologians, added to the fact that when traditions in which he figures did commence to appear he was commonly identified in them with the Christian Messiah,[31] makes it plain that the Mahdī is only a late invention modelled on, and intended to parallel, the Christian expectation of the Second Advent of Jesus. To many pious Muslims it must have seemed passing strange that the figure of Jesus should have so large a part in the accounts of the events of the Last Days, while that of their

---

[25] Arthur in Avalon, Ogier the Dane, Barbarossa in the Kyffhäusser are only three examples among many. See F. Kampers, *Die Deutsche Kaiseridee in Prophetie und Sage* (München, 1896), and *Vom Werdegang der abendländischen Kaisermystik* (Berlin, 1924).

[26] Hans Schmidt, *Der Mythos vom wiederkehrenden König im Alten Testament*, 1913.

[27] IV Ezra, VI, 26. For Enoch see I Enoch, XC, 31: *Hist. Jos. Carp*, §§ 31, 32: *Gosp. Nicod.*, § 25. For Elijah see Sirach, XLVIII, 10; Mark, IX, 11; *Orac. Sibyl.*, II, 155 ff.; *Exod. Rabba*, III, 12; *Eduyot*, VIII, 7; *Pesaḥ*, 13 a; *Menah.*, 45 a. For Moses see *Targ. Yer.* to Deut., XXXIII, 21; *Deut. Rabba*, XI, 9, 10.

[28] Gaster, *Asatir*, pp. 103 ff.

[29] *Yasht*, XIII, 129; XIX, 89; *Bundahish*, XXX, 1–22; *Dinkart*, IX, 23.

[30] Mrs. Drower, *Mandaeans of Iraq*, p. 8, quotes this from a MS of *Haran Gawaitha*, but I have not seen the text.

[31] The common statement is, "There is no Mahdī save Jesus son of Mary." See *Kanz*, VII, No. 1932; Pseudo-Balkhī, II, 181.

own Prophet Muḥammad played no part at all. The Mahdī was their answer to this problem. His coming precedes the Descent of Jesus, and as we have already seen, some Traditions say that it is behind him that Jesus will say prayers the moment he descends.[32] With the Mahdī also is associated a period of opulence and Millennial bliss.[33] Indeed, many of the traditions concerning him closely parallel those telling of the doings of Jesus at his descent,[34] and it is curious that when the writers reach the account of the arrival of the Judgment Day and the description of the Grand Assizes and its sequents, in which Muḥammad appears to exercise his role as general Intercessor, the figure of the Mahdī fades out completely, though both those of Jesus and Muḥammad continue to play a part throughout the Grand Assizes and into the life of eternity.

B. *The Beast*

The Beast is mentioned in the Qur'ān. In XXVII, 82/84 we read:

> And when the sentence has fallen on them We shall cause to come forth to them from the earth a Beast, which will speak with them. Truly the people were not convinced of Our signs.

The "sentence" here would seem to be the sentence passed on men at the Judgment, after the accounting before the Judge, so that one wonders if Muḥammad, who speaks so often about the "Balances" at the accounting, had not in mind the monstrous beast

[32] Pseudo-Balkhī, II, 191, 192; ash-Sha'rānī, *Tadhkira*, p. 118.

[33] 'Alī al-Qārī, V, 180; *Kanz*, VII, Nos. 1976 and 1945; Ahmad b.Hanbal, *Musnad*, III, 37, 52.

[34] Some even make him share with Jesus in the slaying of ad-Dajjāl. See ash-Sha'rānī, p. 118, and the discussion in Attema, *De mohammedaansche Opvattingen omtrent het Tijdstip van den Jongsten Dag en zijn Voorteekenen*, Amsterdam, 1942, p. 167.

who squats beside the Balances in the Egyptian pictures of the soul's accounting. The Commentators, however, are agreed that the Beast is an accompaniment of the approaching Hour, and so it figures among the Signs of the Hour. It is said to be a composite beast made up of parts of various animals.[35] It will come out from a place in the desert near Mecca, bringing with it the rod of Moses and the seal of Solomon.[36] With the rod it will make resplendent the faces of the believers so that they appear white, and with the seal it will put a stamp on the nose of every unbeliever so that his face becoms black.[37] There is some uncertainty among them as to when the Beast will appear. Some say that it will come forth while the Mahdī is among men, though others say not till Jesus has killed ad-Dajjāl,[38] and yet others say that the Beast will not come till after the Abyssinians have wrecked the Kaʿba at Mecca, which would make its coming the last of all the seven greater signs.

The correspondences between certain details in these Traditions about the Beast and the account in Rev. 13 are too close to leave any doubt that though the Muḥammadan figure of the Beast may contain features which survived in popular thought from a very ancient myth of combat with a monster,[39] yet as it took its

[35] az-Zamakhsharī, *al-Kashshāf*, p. 1038; Pseudo-Balkhī, II, 198, 199. So the beast *Āmām* or *Ām-mit*, the "eater of the dead" in the Papyrus of Ani, is a composite beast.

[36] az-Zamakhsharī, p. 1039; Aḥmad b.Ḥanbal, *Musnad*, II, 491; *Kanz*, VII, Nos. 2164, 2998; Pseudo-Balkhī, II, 199.

[37] Some say that it will mark the word "Believer" on the faces of the one group and the word "Unbeliever" on the faces of the other.

[38] See Attema's discussion on pp. 140–142. al-Bisṭāmī quoted by Rüling, *Beiträge zur Eschatologie des Islam*, p. 49, said that Jesus would descend while ad-Dajjāl was besieging the Mahdī in Jerusalem. This seems to be a harmonizing Tradition attempting to bring the two figures together. Rüling himself suggests that the Muslims have identified the Mahdī with the Rabbinic Messias ben Joseph, and the descending Jesus with the expected Messias ben David.

[39] Söderblom, *La vie future*, p. 303, notes how the ethnic myth of a primitive combat with a monstrous beast tends to get transferred to the pictures of the Endzeit. His two examples are the *Aži Dahāk* of the *Avesta* and the Fenrer wolf of the *Edda*, but there are many parallels.

place in the eschatological picture of the End it was a confused reminiscence of the Beast of the Apocalypse.[40]

C. *The Anti-Christ*

Ad-Dajjāl, the Anti-Christ, is another composite figure.[41] He is a combination of the figures of the false Prophet who appears with the Beast in Rev. 19:20, the devil of Rev. 20:7, the deceiver who precedes Gog and Magog, the Beasts in Rev. 13, and the "man of sin" of II Thess. 2:3–12. This figure very quickly attracted to itself all the characteristics of the False Messiah and of the Anti-Christ current in Jewish and Christian legend, as well as those associated with Beliar, so that he came to be particularly associated with the Great Apostasy (or Decay of Faith), and the Great Tribulation, which precede the End. He will come riding on a donkey, will set himself up to be as God, claiming men's allegiance, working mighty miracles, and bringing with him mountains of food and rivers of wine. He will promise Paradise and Hell, will greatly afflict true believers, deceive many of the righteous, and have an extraordinary attraction for women, Jews, and hypocrites.[42]

There is no mention of him in the Qur'ān but he appears in the earliest stratum of Tradition. 'Ā'isha, the Prophet's girl wife, used to say:

The Prophet's invocation (*du'ā*) in his daily prayers was: "Allahumma! I take refuge with Thee from three things only; from the torments of the tomb, from the distress of *al-masīḥ ad-dajjāl*, and from the distresses of life and death" (*Mishkāt*, pp. 87, 216; *Kanz*, VII, No. 2987),

[40] Tor Andrae, *Der Ursprung des Islams und das Christentum*, p. 63. It is perhaps noteworthy that the two beasts of Rev. 13 have been combined in the Muslim traditions.

[41] He is discussed by Attema on pp. 52–56, 113–133, 177–179.

[42] *Kanz*, VII, Nos. 2023–2082, 2116; Pseudo-Balkhī, II, 188, 189; 'Alī al-Qārī, V, 190–212.

and Abū Huraira, one of Muḥammad's Companions, reported that the Prophet used to insist that he was warning his community against ad-Dajjāl because there had been no Prophet since the days of Noah who had not warned his community against him.[43] One of the most widely known Traditions concerning him reads:

Nawwār b.Sam'ān said that the Apostle of Allah made mention of ad-Dajjāl, saying: "If he comes forth while I am with you, I shall be your *hajīj* [defender] against him, but if he comes forth when I am no longer among you, then every man must be his own *hajīj*, though Allah is my *Khalīfa* [vicegerent] over every Muslim. He will be a young man [*shābb*], with curly hair and a floating eye, resembling 'Abd al-'Uzzā b.Qaṭan [a local youth]. If anyone meets him let him recite against him the beginning of Sūra XVIII, for that is a protection against his distresses. He will come forth from a gap between Syria and al-'Irāq, making mischief to right and to left. So, O servants of Allah, be firm." We said: "O Apostle of Allah, how long will he remain on earth?" He said: "Forty days. One day will be like a year, one day like a month, one day like a week, and the rest just days like yours." We said: "O Apostle of Allah, on that day that is like a year shall we make do with one day's prayer services?" He said: "No! Give it its due measure." We said: "O Apostle of Allah, how fast will he move in the earth?" He said: "Like rain which the wind drives along. He will come to a people and summon them, and they will believe on him, so he will command the heavens and they will rain on the earth, which will produce such vegetation that their cattle will return in the evening large of hump, full-uddered and fat of flank. Then he will come to another people and summon them, but they will reject his words, so he will turn from them and in the morning they will be famine stricken with none of their possessions left. He will pass by a ruined place and say to it—Bring forth your treasures! whereat its treasures will follow him like bees in a swarm. Then he will call a man, a youth, whom he will smite

---

[43] *Kanz*, VII, No. 2039; al-Bukhārī, *Ṣaḥīḥ*, IV, 453; Aḥmad b.Ḥanbal, *Musnad*, I, 195, II, 135.

with a sword so as to cut him into two sections an arrow's distance apart. Then he will summon him, and he will come to life, and go to him with joyful face and full of laughter. While he is thus Allah will send Jesus." [44]

The majority of Traditions tell how he will flee from Jesus when he sees him, but Jesus will pursue him, overtake him at the gate of Lydda, and kill him there.[45] Then the true believers will make slaughter of his followers.[46] This is the first great work of Jesus after his Descent, a great work of deliverance, for the Prophet had said:

"From the creation of Adam to the hour of the Last Judgment there is no greater calamity than the appearance of ad-Dajjāl." [47]

When he is removed from earth the end is very near. There is a *ḥadīth* according to which Muḥammad was asked which would come first, ad-Dajjāl or Jesus, and he answered:

"ad-Dajjāl and then Jesus, and then were a man to assist a mare to bring forth her colt, he would not ride that colt ere the Hour is at hand" (*Kanz*, VII, Nos. 2973, 2975).

D. *Gog and Magog*

In that interval, however, between Jesus and the End, Gog and Magog come forth.[48] They break through the wall that Alexander the Great had set up to keep them back, as is related in the

[44] *Mishkāt*, p. 473; *Kanz*, VII, No. 2026.
[45] *Kanz*, VII, No. 2119; Aḥmad b.Ḥanbal, *Musnad*, VI, 75; al-Bīrūnī, *Chronologie*, p. 212, and see the *Qāmūs* s.v. *Ludd*. It is curious that in the Rabbinic texts Ben Stada, who many think represents Simon Magus, is also to be destroyed at Lydda. *Sanh.*, 67 a; *Yer. Sanh.*, VII, 16; *Tos. Sanh.*, x, 11.
[46] *Kanz*, VII, No. 2028; Pseudo-Balkhī, II, 191; Nuwairī, *Nihāya*, XIV, 283.
[47] 'Alī al-Qārī, V, 189; Pseudo-Balkhī, II, 193; *Mishkāt*, p. 473.
[48] See Attema's discussion on pp. 56, 134–140.

Qur'ān,⁴⁹ and march down into the Holy Land, destroying everything in their path.⁵⁰ Then Jesus performs his second act of deliverance by rescuing the faithful remnant who have been preserved from ad-Dajjāl and sheltering them in aṭ-Ṭūr.⁵¹ When they reach the environs of Jerusalem the hosts of Gog and Magog will say:

"We have conquered all the peoples of the earth; now let us attack the heavens. So they will shoot their arrows against it, and Allah will send them back covered with blood. Then they will imagine that they have finished off the inhabitants of the heavens and so boast of their victory over all on earth and all in the heavens that the Believers will say to Jesus: 'O Spirit of Allah, pray for their annihilation.' So Jesus will pray to Allah against them, whereat Allah will send little white worms which will enter their ears and kill them all in one night." ⁵²

The third act of deliverance on the part of Jesus is his prayer which brings about the cleansing of the earth from the stench of their corpses, as already related.

Some say that it is now that Jesus ushers in the Millennial period of peace and prosperity, though more commonly this is thought to have occupied the interval between the killing of ad-Dajjāl and the coming of Gog and Magog. In Muslim thought this is not a

⁴⁹ Sūra, XVIII, 93/92 ff. Verse 98 states that when Allah is ready the wall is obliterated, and v. 99, which is usually taken to be a continuation of this passage, though apparently it was not so originally, speaks of the blowing of the Trump at the Last Day, so it was an easy step for later Islamic thought to link the Qur'ānic Gog and Magog with the Judaeo-Christian teaching about their place in the events of the Endzeit.

⁵⁰ Ibn Qayyim, *Kitāb ar-Rūḥ*, p. 25; *Kanz*, VII, Nos. 2026, 2939; Aḥmad b. Ḥanbal, *Musnad*, I, 375.

⁵¹ *Mishkāt*, p. 473; *Kanz*, VII, Nos. 1921, 3021; Nuwairī, *Nihāya*, XIV, 278.

⁵² *Kanz*, VII, No. 2939. Cf. Pseudo-Balkhī, II, 206 and Aḥmad b.Ḥanbal, *Musnad*, IV, 181. In Rabbinic writings we find that the Messiah was expected to lead in the war against Gog and Magog. See IV Ezra, XIII, 32; *Targ. Yer.* to Numb., XXIV, 17, 20.

thousand-year period, but a relatively brief period, and in it Jesus fulfils the other functions of his descent.

(1) Since he did not marry when he was on earth the first time, he now marries and becomes a family man.[53]

(2) Since on his first coming among men he refused to act as a judge among them, he now takes official position as a leader of the faithful, and since the true faithful are Muslims he now acts as a pious Muslim.[54] He will pray and will lead prayers in Muslim fashion, will break the crosses and kill swine, both of which are offensive things to Muslims.[55] He will perform the pilgrimage to Mecca,[56] and visit the tomb of Muḥammad [57] at Madina. He will rule the faithful according to the *sharīʿa* (the Muḥammadan religious law),[58] and will undertake the task of converting to Islam all the peoples left on earth,[59] a task in which he will be so successful that he is said to abolish the *jizya* (poll-tax), since there will be no non-Muslims left on whom it could be levied.[60] This is the great conversion predicted by Muḥammad:

[53] as-Suyūtī, *Durar*, p. 19; *Mishkāt*, pp. 479, 480; ash-Shaʿrānī, *Tadhkira*, p. 133; ʿAlī al-Qārī, V, 223.

[54] Some Traditions say that he will call to the people who had fled into hiding from the persecution under ad-Dajjāl, and they will come out to him, so that he assembles all the faithful under him. *Kanz*, VII, No. 2104; Nuwairī, *Nihāya*, XIV, 277.

[55] ʿAlī al-Qārī, V, 221, 222; *Mishkāt*, 479, 480; al-Baiḍāwī on Sūra, XLIII, 61; *Kanz*, VII, No. 3010.

[56] *Kanz*, VI, No. 1969, and cf. VII, No. 3009; ash-Shaʿrānī, p. 133.

[57] ash-Shaʿrānī, p. 138; *Kanz*, VII, No. 2137.

[58] Muḥammad had said that when Jesus came down he would be a just *hakam*, and this was taken to mean that he would govern the community according to the Muslim *sharīʿa*. See al-Bukhārī, *Ṣaḥīḥ*, II, 370; *Kanz*, VII, No. 3015; al-Faḍālī, *Kifāyat al-ʿAwāmm*, p. 138.

[59] *Kanz*, VII, No. 2141. The general way of stating it is to say that all religions save Islam will perish in his day (as-Suyūtī, *Durar*, 19; ash-Shaʿrānī, p. 133), but al-Baiḍāwi commenting on Sūra, XLIII, 61, goes so far as to say that Jesus will kill off all the Christians who do not accept this new position which he has taken with regard to religion.

[60] al-Baijūrī, *Taḥqīq*, p. 138, discusses the theological problems raised by this.

In his day [i.e., after the descent of Jesus] Allah will put an end to all religions (*milal*) save Islam.[61]

(3) Since he did not die at his first advent he will now die, the Muslims will pray over him according to Islamic ritual for burial, and he will be buried at Madina beside the grave of Muḥammad.[62]

His death, however, will not be solitary; it will be part of the Rapture. While he is at Madina Allah will send a perfumed breeze from Paradise, which will waft away the soul of Jesus along with the souls of all true believers, so that only those who were not true believers, who had made but a pretense of religion, will be left alive on earth to witness the tribulation of the last two signs, and hear the Blast of Consternation, the first of the Trumps, which announces that the Last Day has arrived. One form of this Tradition reads:

> While they are thus Allah will send an odoriferous wind which will seize them under the armpits, and the soul of every

[61] *Kanz*, VII, No. 2128. This idea of a great conversion is a common one in eschatology. The Rabbis believed that in the last days there would be a great turning to the religion of Israel, for were there not the promises of Isa., II, 2 ff.; LXVI, 19 ff.; Dan. VII, 14; Zech. VIII, 21–23; XIV, 9, 16 ff.? Cf. I Enoch, X, 21; XC, 30; *Orac. Siby.*, III, 702 ff.; Tobit, XIII, 10–18; XIV, 4–6; *'Aboda zara*, 24 a. The Zoroastrian *Bahman Yasht*, III, 47–49, teaches that when Hūšēdār appears all mankind will be converted to the Mazdaean religion, and the Samaritans held that when the Tāheb came all men would be converted to their faith (*Shīra Yetima*, p. 513; *Molad Mosheh*, p. 345.)

[62] *Kanz*, VII, Nos. 2128, 2141, 2142, 2939. 'Ā'isha is said to have asked if she could not be buried beside Muḥammad, but he answered her that he had no control over that matter, for there were but three places for tombs beside his, those of her father Abū Bakr and of 'Umar, and the one reserved for Jesus (*Kanz*, VII, No. 3017). Sir Richard Burton in his *Pilgrimage to al-Madinah*, I, 325, tells about its place there in modern days.

It is noteworthy that two others who were taken to heaven without death, viz. Enoch and Elijah, are popularly supposed to be the "two witnesses" who precede the coming of ad-Dajjāl to warn the people against him, and are killed in the troubles during the triumphant days of the Anti-Christ (cf. Aḥmad b.Ḥanbal, *Musnad*, V, 221). The explanation usually given is that since Allah has said in the Qur'ān (III, 185/182), "every soul shall taste of death," those who escaped death by translation must return and die and be partakers in the general resurrection.

true believer, every Muslim, will be taken, and the wicked will
be left, wantoning on the earth like asses, so that it is upon
them that the Hour will come,[63]

while another says:

Then will Allah send a perfumed wind and it will take off
the soul of everyone in whose heart there is as much faith as
a grain of mustard seed, so there will remain only those in
whom is no good, who will return to the religion of their
fathers [i.e., to paganism].[64]

This initiating the Rapture is the final deliverance wrought by
Jesus after his descent.

It will have been noticed how numerous are the points of con-
tact between this Muslim account of the Descent of Jesus and the
popular Judaeo-Christian accounts of the work of the Messiah
during the Last Days. In the *Sibylline Oracles*, III, 652–818, for
example, we have an account of the coming of the Messiah, in
which we read how God will send him from the East to put an
end to civil war, slaying some and fulfilling the promises on behalf
of others, but being rightly guided in all things by God, so that
the Temple will be resplendent with glory and the earth teem with
fruitfulness. The evil nations will then muster their forces and
attack Palestine, but God will destroy them, and their judgment
will be accompanied by fearful portents. Israel, however, in those
days will dwell safely under divine protection, and then the rest
of the cities and islands will be converted so as to unite with Israel
in praising God. The blessings of the Messianic age are then re-
counted. This is only one example from among many where the
correspondences are so close as to leave no escape from the conclusion that the Jews and Christians who, in the early years of

---

[63] *Kanz*, VII, No. 2026; *Mishkāt*, p. 474; 'Alī al-Qārī, V, 200, 201; Nuwairī, *Nihāya*, XIV, 279.

[64] *Kanz*, VII, No. 1708; 'Alī al-Qārī, V, 277; Aḥmad b.Ḥanbal, *Musnad*,
II, 166; III, 420; IV, 182.

Islam, became Muslims, brought into their new religion a great deal of the teaching familiar to them about the place the Messiah would have in the events of the Last Days. Then, as eschatological thought developed within Islam, Christian teaching in particular contributed greatly to that development. Tor Andrae, in his Uppsala essay *Der Ursprung des Islams und das Christentum* in 1926, pointed out how closely the eschatology of the Qur'ān corresponds with that of the Syriac-speaking Church. One could similarly illustrate point by point all we have discussed above concerning the Descent of Jesus from the writings of these same writers both Nestorian and Jacobite.

The precise sources from which these Christian influences entered Islamic thought is not, however, a matter of much importance. What is more important is the fact that though Muḥammad himself definitely rejected the idea of a Redeemer, the Islamic community has felt deeply the need of such a Redeemer, and has in various ways sought to introduce one into the Islamic system. Sometimes they have endeavored to make Muḥammad himself a redeemer, and sometimes his son-in-law 'Alī (or members of 'Alī's family). Here, however, in the eschatological picture we find the figure of Jesus appearing as a redeemer; not such a Redeemer as he is thought of in Christian faith and proves himself to be in Christian experience, but within the frame of reference of the Islamic faith exercising his redemptive office on behalf of the Muslim community itself, to whom he is then the Elect even among the elect.

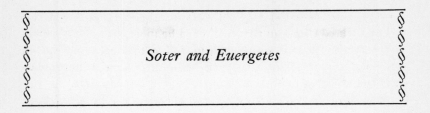

Soter and Euergetes

by ARTHUR DARBY NOCK
Harvard University

Frederick C. Grant, as writer, teacher, editor, and translator, has laid students of the New Testament under a heavy debt, and we must all hope that he will long be spared to make the debt yet heavier. On this happy occasion I can offer in return only a token payment, in the shape of a few remarks on two ancient expressions of gratitude which have their place in the New Testament.

I

Soter was a word which took much of its color from its context. It could be used of gods and men alike and, when applied to the latter, it did not necessarily suggest that they belonged or approximated to the category of the former. We have to ask this question each time: who was the deliverer and from what did he give deliverance? So the Septuagint uses *soter* not only of God but also of individual leaders and of Mordecai (in relation to the king),[1] and Hyperides said that it was necessary for the upright

[1] Cf. G. Bertram in G. Kittel, *Theo. Wörterb.* II, p. 652; Nock, *Class. Phil.* XLIII (1948), p. 123, and in *Essays on the Trinity and the Incarnation*, ed. A. E. J. Rawlinson, pp. 87ff. (For Septuagint use add II Esdr. 19:27; cf. σώζειν of Samson, Judges 13:5). A comparable problem is presented by the words *princeps* and *auctoritas*; cf. H. Last, *J. Rom. Stud.* XL (1950), pp. 119 ff.

leader of the people to be the *soter* of his fatherland; [2] now it is not to be expected of a man that he should be more than a man. *Soter* so used did not involve any such metaphor as is to be seen with *pater* and with *theos* (whether used absolutely or with a genitive or dative, "god of or for *x* or *y*").[3]

The earliest known applications of *soter* are to gods; Zeus Soter, Artemis Soteira, Athena Soteira were firmly entrenched in usage. Yet if the application of *soter* to men involved a transfer, this was early and unconscious, for Aesch. *Suppl.* 980 has no suggestion of hyperbole.[4] "We should pray and offer sacrifices and libations to the Argives, just as to Olympian gods, for they are undoubtedly our *soteres*"; this applies to the Argives as a whole, not to their king alone, and there was no more possibility of imputing divinity to the Argives in general than to the Romans. Further, Aeschylus was an intense theist, writing in the heyday of the older piety before it had been subjected to any of the solvents of rationalism.

[2] P. 11 ed. Jensen (the letters σω and the word "fatherland" are supplied, but the sense is clear). Cf. Dio Prus. XXXII 3, and "able to save" in Plat. *Laws*, 962B; L. Delatte, *Les traités de la Royauté d'Ecphante, Diotogène et Sthénidas*, pp. 249 f. It can be the duty of a king to imitate God or a god, but not to be such.

[3] Cf. M. P. Charlesworth, *Harv. Theol. Rev.* XXVIII (1935), pp. 12f., with a significant quotation from Philo *V. Mos.* I, 158 (add *Q. omn. pr. lib.*, 43, with Colson's note, and *Somn.* I, 228 ff.; in 230 I should for once modify Colson's wonderful version and read: "Since it does not suffer from any overscrupulous anxiety about an impropriety in its choice of words.") Cf. also John 10:34 f. and P. Mich. 209:13 (in J. G. Winter, *Michigan Papyri*, III, p. 267). For a slightly more formal use of "*theos* and *kyrios*," copied from royal style, cf. *Harv. Theol. Rev.* XXIX (1936), p. 50.

[4] The reply of the Chorus begins (1014), "May the Olympian gods give us luck in other respects"; the situation is in the hands of the gods. So in *Choeph.* 264, Orestes and Electra are called *soteres*. When the Athenian settlers on Lemnos used the formula "of Seleucus *soter*" over a cup of wine at a symposion (Phylarch. *ap.* Athenae. 255A), they were naturally alluding to the regular "of Zeus *soter*" (J. Kaerst, *Gesch.* II, ed. 2, p. 318); this was in the experimental period of homage to kings. *Contra*, "third *soter*" of a Spartan sage in Plato, *Laws* 692A is a metaphorical way of describing the third stage of the city's being made secure.

Three points may be added. First, we know little of the forms of daily speech of an earlier time; how did devoted adherents speak of Pisistratus? Secondly, the words which Aeschylus puts in the mouth of Danaus simply give a particular formulation to the sentiment expressed by Odysseus to Nausicaa in Odyssey VIII, 464 ff.[5] and (in hopeful anticipation of a kindness) to the stranger who proves to be Athena in disguise (*ib.* XIII, 230 f.). Thirdly, *soter* does no more than crystallize the sense of the verb *sozo*; the earlier *saoo*, like *rhyomai*, was freely used in Homer of men and gods alike (cf. n. 32). As Professor Sterling Dow has reminded me, Aristotle speaks of Solon as having saved Athens (*Ath. Pol.* 11); some contemporaries may have done likewise.

Zeus, as father of men and gods, was strong to aid; Artemis protected women in childbirth; Athena guarded the Acropolis and might be thought willing and able to help in countless ways. In fact, any deity was credited with powers which men lacked,[6] and could aid as humanity could not. But man was able to do his part. A king or leader had more scope than a commoner and the Emperor Titus had more chance than John Doe of doing his daily good deed and could do it on a larger scale; the fact of power could be ennobled by the gospel of service.[7] Yet there were humbler counterparts, in the good turns done in daily life, and these might even be thought to merit the use of the term *theos*.[8]

Soter had a wide range of meaning and emphasis in paganism. It was one thing when used to express the gratitude or hopes or promises of a moment, another thing when accorded or assumed as a constant epithet.[9] But at all times it denoted the performance

[5] Charlesworth, *l.c.*, p. 8.
[6] Cf. Liv. I, 24.8 *tantoque magis ferito quanto magis potes pollesque.*
[7] Cf. Cic. *Ligar.* 38; Plin. *N.H.* II, 18.
[8] Cf. *Ep. ad Diognet.* 10.6.
[9] Cf. W. W. Tarn, *Greeks in Bactria and India*, p. 175 (on Apollodotus and Menander as taking the title *soter* when wishing to be regarded as deliverers; also p. 204). So again, while many deities had *soter* as a regular epithet, it could be applied to others *ad hoc*, e.g., to a river-god who was

of a function and not membership of a class in the hierarchy of beings.[10]

Four pieces of evidence after Alexander's time might be thought to tell against this view. First, a decree of the League of Islanders, passed about 280 B.C., states that it is appropriate that the League should take its part in the festival recently established for Ptolemy I by Ptolemy II at Alexandria, since they had taken the lead in honoring the *soter* Ptolemy (i.e., Ptolemy I) with honors equal to the divine because of his benefactions in general and the kindnesses which they in particular had received.[11] This has sometimes been taken to indicate that the title *soter* itself was what was meant by these "honors," but it is far more likely that the reference is to sacrifices, such as the Islanders offered a little later "to the other gods and to Ptolemy Soter and to king Ptolemy" (i.e., Ptolemy II).[12] The text under consideration had earlier spoken of Ptolemy I as "king and *soter*" (ll. 10 f.; cf. 43 f.) and later it mentions the "altar of Ptolemy *soter*" (ll. 48 f.) and prescribes that the members should set this decision on stone in the temples in which

---

thought to have relieved a plague: *I(nscriptiones) G(raecae ad) R(es) R(omanas pertinentes)* IV, 1389.

[10] E. Skard, *Avh. Norske Akad.*, 1931, ii, p. 28, remarks that in classical times *soter* was used of men who were not heroized but were set above common humanity. H. Kleinknecht, *Arch. f. Rel.-Wiss.* XXXIV (1937), p. 307, finds in *soter* etc. in Old Comedy a parody of *Gottmenschentum*. But the only known clear *Gottmenschentum* of the period was that of Empedocles, and we have to consider the evidence of the usage in tragedy. As for the hero of the Birds, we must remember the old myth that Zeus had dethroned Kronos and had himself to face the danger of being supplanted, and C. Bonner's suggestion, *Am. J. Phil.* LXIV (1943), pp. 208 ff. (In the story quoted by K. from Timaeus *ap.* Athen. 37E, the drunken men thought of possible deliverers as doing for them what the Dioscuri were deemed to do for those literally in peril at sea).

[11] Dittenberger, *Syll. inscr. gr.* (ed. 3), 390.26 ff. Cf. W. W. Tarn, *Antigonos Gonatas*, pp. 438 f. and *Camb. Anc. Hist.* VII, p. 101. For the phrase cf. Dittenberger 624.4, where it refers to the cult of Philopoemen as it was to be established; also n. 37.

[12] P. Roussel, *Bull. Corr. Hell.* 1907, pp. 340 ff.

the other honors were already recorded (ll. 51 ff.). That Ptolemy I
was appropriately described as Soter (the initiative in doing this
was traditionally ascribed to the Rhodians) is, so to speak, taken
for granted. The phrase is far less marked than the Athenian desig-
nation and description, a quarter of a century earlier, of Antigonus
and Demetrius as *hoi Soteres* without any feeling that personal
names were needed.[13]

Secondly, Cicero says in his published indictment of Verres:

> Itaque eum non solum PATRONUM illius insulae sed etiam SOTERA
> inscriptum vidi Syracusis. Hoc quantum est? Ita magnum ut Latine
> uno verbo exprimi non possit. Is est nimirum Soter qui salutem
> dedit. Huius nomine etiam dies festi agitantur, pulcra illa Verria,
> non quasi Marcellia, sed pro Marcelliis, quae illi istius iussu sus-
> tulerunt.[14]

Cicero is stating, with studied irony, what might be thought to be
indications of the affection of the provincials for their oppressor.
He does not return to the point, as he does to the institution of
the Verria [15] and the gilded statues of Verres,[16] nor does he suggest that *soter* was divine or quasi-divine (not that he would have
regarded such a tribute from Greeks as improper).[17] He simply
concentrates on the exotic character of the term, as being more
than the normal *patronus* and as having no full equivalent in Latin
—and that although he himself later used *servator* and *conservator*

---

[13] W. S. Ferguson, *Hesperia* XVII (1948), pp. 114, 136; cf. U. Wilcken,
Sitzungsber. Berlin, 1938, p. 309, on Ptolemy I as *theos soter* at Ptolemais, and
θεὸς οἵα σαωτήρ in a text composed by a contemporary of Plutarch (J. H.
Oliver, *Hesperia, Supp.* VIII, p. 246).

[14] *In Verr.* II, ii, 154.

[15] *Ib.* 51, 52, 114; cf. iv 24, 151, *deorum honores.*

[16] *Ib.* 50, 114.

[17] Cf. *ib.* 51 *debitum reddebant,* which is parallel to the phrase *legitimum
honorem* in Liv. XXXII 25.4, discussed by C. F. Edson, *Harv. Theol. Rev.*
XXVI (1933), pp. 324 f. *Ad Q. fratr.* I, 1.31 is often quoted; but D. Magie,
Roman Rule in Asia Minor, p. 1244, has expressed doubts as to the authenticity of the letter and they will require consideration. (In favor of the letter
cf. M. I. Henderson, *J. Rom. Stud.* XL, 1950, p. 16.)

in a similar sense.[18] His language is ironical, like Tertullian's use of *soter*, in *Adv. Valentin.* 12.[19] That is, I think, all.

Thirdly, Germanicus, in his edict of 19 A.D. to the Alexandrians, says:

"I welcome your good will which you show on each occasion when you see me. But I altogether deprecate acclamations of yours which are for me invidious and which belong to the level of divinity (*isotheous*), for they are suitable only for him who is really the *soter* and *euergetes* (benefactor) of the whole human race, that is, my father, and for his mother, who is my grandmother. I am only a servant of their divinity. So, if you do not

[18] For *conservator*, of a private individual, cf. *Corp. inscr. lat.* IX, 1033 and perhaps V, 3422. Mr. Zeph Stewart draws my attention to Sen. *Ben.* II, 18.8, *si servasti me, non ideo servator es,* as a passage in which *servator* is specific. Liv. VI, 17.5, has *Selibrisne farris gratiam servatori patriae relatam? Et quem prope caelestem, cognomine certe Capitolino Iovi parem fecerint* . . . ; but the *cognomen* in question is Capitolinus as bestowed on Manlius.

On the Latinization of *soter* cf. A. Oxé, *Wien. St.* XLVIII (1930), pp. 38 ff.; Chr. Mohrmann, *Vig. Christ.* IV (1950), p. 202; n. 78 later. Salus, which Cicero uses in his circumlocution, sometimes corresponds to Hygieia (with our small or capital letter). Now Hygieia, when personified, was more specific than *soteria* and, thanks to association with Asclepius, acquired an individuality and an art-type. Salus also was so represented, but at Rome remained more general; her temple at Rome was vowed by a consul during a Samnite war (Liv. IX 43.25), not during a plague. So in Plautus the character who promises to help another out of a difficulty and could well have been *soter* in Greek is called or calls himself Salus (e.g., *Asin.* 712 ff.), *Spes, Salus, Victoria* (Merc. 867; cf. Wissowa in Roscher, *Lex. Myth.* IV, col. 295). The second phrase, like *ego nunc tibi sum summus Iuppiter, idem ego sum Salus, Fortuna, Lux, Laetitia, Gaudium* (*Capt.* 863 f.) may well be a Plautine elaboration (cf. Ed. Fraenkel, *Plautinisches im Plautus,* p. 225). Does such language help us to understand what Michael Grant (*Num. Chron.* 1949, p. 22 ff. and *Univ. Edinburgh Journal,* Spring 1949, pp. 229 ff.) has called the complex symbolism of Roman Imperial coinage? The coinage was trying to set forth the richness of blessings vouchsafed to mankind in and through wise and beneficent rule. (For the complexity cf. Dessau, *Inscr. lat. sel.* 8063b and the priesthood of *Providentia Aug.* and *Salus publica* established at Corinth—possibly to commemorate the overthrow of Sejanus: A. B. West, *Corinth,* VIII, ii, pp. 14 and 90, no. 110.)—Conversely, an inscription from Caria published by A. Laumonier, *Bull. Corr. Hell.,* 1934, pp. 300 ff., has the title, "priest of the Hygieia and Soteria of the Emperor"; the double phrase seems to correspond to *Salus Augusta* (or *Augusti*).

[19] Mohrmann, *l.c.,* p. 204.

follow my wishes, you will compel me not to appear before you often." [20]

The language here follows a pattern, which may well be Augustan, for the refusal at will of extravagant honors when directly offered,[21] and Germanicus speaks of Tiberius and Livia somewhat as, in the Gytheum edict, Tiberius speaks of Augustus.[22]

Yet there is a difference. The pattern of refusal was pertinent when something formal was proffered by a community acting as such, not when there had been nothing more than popular huzzas. On the face of it, Germanicus describes the epithets *soter* and *euer-*

[20] Wilamowitz-Zucker, *Sitzungsber. Berlin,* 1911, pp. 794 ff., and Hunt-Edgar, *Select Papyri,* II, p. 76, no. 211, with U. Wilcken, *Herm.* LXIII (1928), pp. 48 ff. I accept G. Kalbfleisch's reading ἐν ὑπηρεσίᾳ (*ib.* LXXVII, 1942, pp. 374 ff.) rather than L. A. Post's ἔνλογα παρεπ(όμενα) (*Am. J. Phil.* LXV, 1944, pp. 80 ff.). The general sense is clear. In the hippodrome at Alexandria the newly designated emperor Vespasian was greeted with the more emphatic εἰς σωτὴρ καὶ εὐεργέτης (P. Jouguet, *Mél. Ernout,* p. 202).

[21] Cf. M. P. Charlesworth, *Pap. Brit. Sch. Rome,* XV (1939), pp. 1 ff. He quotes an instance of a Roman accepting *euergetes* and refusing *ktistes*; others were less sensitive. *Ktistes,* though dignified and applicable to superhuman beings, had in itself nothing savoring of the divine, but the principle of modesty sometimes caused men to reject such tributes; cf. *I.G.R.R.* III, 739, viii, 99 ff. (with the same παραιτεῖσθαι and ἀρχεῖσθαι). So in *Eur. Hipp.* 88 the old Huntsman would not call Hippolytus *despotes*; for the drama, a note of cautious reverence was necessary.

For "invidious" cf. Philostrat. *Ap. Ty.* IV 31, where the hero refuses the celebration of a Theophania "in order that he might not be envied." Ed. Fraenkel follows Wilamowitz in treating Aesch. *Agam.* 925 as an interpolation; if so, it is probably due to a marginal quotation from some other play and certainly reflects common sentiment.

It is instructive to find M. Aurelius and Commodus reverting to the pattern. In a letter to the Sacred Gerousia of Athens father and son declined gold and silver images, saying that they were contented (ἀρχεῖσθαι) with bronze and suggesting busts of portable size should be made; as for terms of honor they deprecated "those that seemed to be invidious" (J. H. Oliver, *Hesperia, Supp.* VI, pp. 108 ff.). We must not forget *Iure caesus* in Suet. *Iul.* 76, after a century and a half of Imperial rule. On Tiberius cf. O. Montevecchi, *Epigraphica,* VII (1945), pp. 104 ff.—Apart from other scruples, it was good form not to let provincials spend too much on statues, etc.: cf. Cic. *Verr.* II 2, 143, *Att.* V 21.7, and Dessau, *Inscr. lat. sel.* 8792.30.

[22] Charlesworth, p. 2.

getes as *isotheous*,[23] but his emphasis is on their invidious character. By common consent the edict was composed with an eye on Tiberius rather than on the Alexandrians. Greater honors had been paid to Germanicus within his sphere of authority and, as we shall see, were from time to time accorded to governors who did not belong to the Imperial house. In Alexandria Germanicus was out of bounds; he had entered Egypt without the permission required for any senator. Antony's grandson must not appear to lend a disloyal ear to the plaudits of irresponsible and often recalcitrant Alexandrians; there must not be even the semblance of a bid for supreme power by a popular and somewhat undisciplined prince, *nimium gaudens popularibus auris.* The epithets in themselves did not matter; their use at Alexandria under the circumstances might. In spite of the similarity of language there is nothing of the high seriousness ascribed to Tiberius in his refusal of a temple in Spain, nothing like Alexander's "It brings peril to the soul" in the A text of Ps.-Callisthenes.[24]

[23] F. de Visscher, *Muséon,* LIX (1946), p. 264, like others, thinks that some title other than *soter* and *euergetes* was meant; against this set the word ὄντως, "really" (so earlier Wilcken, *Arch. Pap. Forsch.* VI, p. 287).

H. Hepding *ap.* M. P. Nilsson, *Gesch. d. griech. Rel.* II, p. 133, remarked that *isotheos* does not put the recipient actually on the level of divinity. (So in the Ptolemaic court the people who were isotimoi or homotimoi with the dignitaries probably ranked after them; cf. Dittenberger, *Or. Gr. Inscr. sel.* 104, n. 2; Liddell-Scott-Jones *s.v.* ἰσότιμος; A. S. F. Gow on Theocr. XVII 16.) In *I.G.R.R.* IV, 1302.15 we read "fitting to the gods and the *issotheoi*" (could *iss.* mean "Julius and Augustus"? Charlesworth translates as "heroes"). In Soph. *Ant.* 834 ff. Niobe is called *theos* and then referred to as belonging to the *isotheoi,* but this is in a lyric intended to console Antigone and the words can hardly be pressed. (Cf. A. Ehrhardt, *Evang. Theol.* 1948, p. 105, on the vulgarization of the epithet.) F. J. Dölger, *Ant. u. Christ.* III (1932), pp. 130 f., has remarked on Christian avoidance of *isotheos,* but Gregory of Nyssa did not shrink from applying it to free will (*P.G.* XLVI, col. 524A), and a Byzantine moralizing poem says "For the king is another god on earth" (V. Lundström, *Anecd. Byz.* I 13, l. 253). We do not find anything like *isheroikos,* since according to tradition a man could attain the dignity of being a heros and the term meant nothing else. (The men who in mythology became gods needed first to be translated.)

[24] II, 22.12, p. 98, ed. Kroll, on which cf. now Tarn, *Alexander the Great,*

Isotheous is so to speak a rhetorical point; in any event, it is here applied to *euergetes* as well as to *soter*. Now *euergetes*, although also applicable to gods and heroes, is a word which clearly has its roots in the human area. In classical times and thereafter it was a regular term in civic decrees to denote a man whose name was thus to be set on stone and recorded as one of a city's benefactors (comparable with the lists of benefactors kept by the Universities of Cambridge and Oxford).[25] It was a less dramatic word than *soter* and could describe continued helpfulness as well as sudden aid in an emergency. In Hellenistic times the category of euergetai received the honor of public sacrifices or games. This involved the putting into practice of a principle which we have seen in Aeschylus, that honors such as were paid to divinity were the highest expression of gratitude. Yet in itself it did not imply any ascription of personal deity to the recipient. This is shown by such a phrase as "to the gods and to the Romans, *euergetai*." [26] The personification of Rome or of the Senate might be

---

II, p. 365. In view of Charlesworth's parallels, we may reject Wilcken's tentative suggestion that this story contains a reminiscence of the Germanicus incident.

[25] For earlier usage cf. Skard, *op. cit.* and *Symb. Oslo.* XXVII (1949), pp. 11 f.; A. Wilhelm, *Sitzungsber. Wien,* CCXX (1942), v, pp. 11 ff.; Nilsson, *Gesch.* II, p. 173. (We await eagerly the study promised by L. Robert, *Hellenica,* IV, p. 131 n.) Contrast the specific *theoi euergetai* of Antony and Octavia at Athens (A. Raubitschek, *Trans. Am. Philol. Ass.* LXXVII, 1946, pp. 146 ff., with a correction by L. Robert, *Rev. ét. gr.* LXI, 1948, pp. 149 f.). For *euergetes* or *soter* and *euergetes* as applied to gods, cf. L. Robert, *Sanctuaire de Sinuri (Mém. inst. fr. d'archéol. de Stamboul,* VII, 1945), pp. 22 ff. Philo applies *euergetes* to God just as he applies such other human predicates as "just," "wise," "good."

[26] Cf. Ch. I. Makaronas, *Epeteris U. Thessalonica,* VI (1948), pp. 293 ff.; J.-L. Robert, *Rev. ét. gr.* LXII (1949), pp. 123 f. Note "to the gods and to the benefactors" (L. Robert, *Bull. Corr. Hell.,* 1926, pp. 499 ff.; cf. his *Ét. Anatol.,* p. 448, n. 3.)

The Greeks had cults of Demokratia or a Demos before they worshipped Roma (Nilsson, II, pp. 136 f.); in a sense, a city could be regarded as immortal. (Cf. Buckler-Calder, *Monum. As. Min. ant.* VI, no. 380, for a priest of the Council and People of Synnada.)

regarded as superhuman; so might an individual Roman of prominence; but the Romans in general could not, any more than the Argives in Aeschylus.

Fourthly, Plutarch, in his *De Alexandri Magni fortuna aut virtute* pours passionate ridicule on the rodomontade of rulers and generals who could not compare with his hero. Some, he says, called themselves *euergetai*, some *kallinikoi* (victorious), some *soteres*, some Great.[27] The selection of epithets and the context show that Plutarch's concern was with pretentiousness in general and not with the arrogation by men of divine attributes as such, against which he protested with vehemence.[28] This is rather the irony of Jesus' words about the "Benefactors" of the Gentiles (Luke 22:25) than the righteous indignation with which the narrator of Acts 12:21 ff. records the gross flattery of Herod by the shouting multitude. Elsewhere Plutarch, when telling how C. Marcius acquired the name Coriolanus, discourses on complimentary epithets in general and says that *soter* and *kallinikos* are epithets given for achievements, and *euergetes* and *philadelphos* for qualities.[29] This is as matter of fact as the statement in a speech put by Dionysius of Halicarnassus in the mouth of Tarquin, that a good king can look forward to being called *euergetes, pater, soter*.[30] Again, Plutarch records without comment the inscription on the base of a bronze statue of Aratus erected at Sicyon by exiles who owed their homecoming to him: "Being restored to our homeland we have, in return for your excellence and justice, set up a representation of you, Aratus, a *soter*, to the gods who are *soteres*." [31] This was a simple statement of the situation, with nothing extravagant in its phrasing.[32]

[27] II 5, p. 338C. Cf. *Aristid.* 6.
[28] K. Scott, *Trans. Am. Philol. Ass.* LX (1929), pp. 117 ff.
[29] *Coriol.* 11.2.
[30] *Ant. Rom.* IV 32.1; cf. Polyb. IX 36.5.
[31] *Arat.* 14; cf. 53.4.
[32] Cf. Eur. *Med.* 476, where Medea says, "I saved you"; 527, Jason's "I think that among deities and men Cypris alone was the *soteira* of my voyag-

Such being the sense and range of *soter*, we need not be surprised to learn from Tacitus that the freedman Milichus took the name Soter after saving Nero from the Pisonian conspiracy.[33] So Herodian represents the officer who denounced Plautianus to Septimius Severus as saying that he came as his *soter* and *euergetes*, and Crispinus as exhorting the soldiers not to betray their loyalty to the Senate and People of Rome but to earn the title of *soteres* and champions of all Italy.[34]

II

When Augustus brought peace and order out of chaos he was deservedly hailed as *soter*, and *soter*, with or without the addition of *euergetes*, was commonly used of later Emperors as a formal predicate (so notably of the great philhellene Hadrian).[35] The wellbeing of a province or of a city depended primarily on the Emperor, and its expressions of gratitude were subject to control.[36] To the best of my knowledge, no temple was erected to a governor later than Actium and no games were created in his honor after those established when the Empire was still young by Mylasa in Caria for C. Marcius Censorinus, probably after his death.[37]

---

ing"; 595, "wishing to save you." Dion of Prusa, in censuring the Alexandrians for that passion for entertainments which caused them to call an artiste *soter* and *theos*, remarks that the gods must laugh in mockery when so addressed by them, "but God is good tempered" (XXXII 50), which is very Greek; cf. *Proc. Am. Philos. Soc.* LXXXV (1942), pp. 472 ff. Dion did not object to the use of *soter* when it was deserved (XLVIII 10).

[33] *Ann.* XV 71.3. *Dio Cass.* LXIII 17.5, says that Nero continually called Corbulo *pater* and *euergetes*; for the combination, cf. Skard, *op. cit.*, pp. 47, 49.
[34] III 12.2; VIII 3.4.
[35] For Hadrian, cf. A. M. Woodward, *Pap. Br. Sch. Ath.* XXVII (1925/6), p. 229, as also (with evidence for Antoninus) XIV (1907/8), p. 139; Oliver, *Hesperia*, X (1941), pp. 249 ff. For Hadrian the epithet is often combined with Zeus Olympios, etc.
[36] *I.G.R.R.* III 704, 745; nn. 48, 73, below.
[37] Lebas-Waddington, *Explication des inscriptions,* pp. 689 f., with the correction of A. W. Persson, *Bull. Corr. Hell.*, 1922, p. 411, and *Supp. Epigr. gr.* II 549. On Censorinus, cf. Münzer in *Pauly-Wissowa*, XIV, cols. 1551 f.

Statues were set up, but as a matter of compliment without cultus.

Nevertheless, *soter*, while most often used of Emperors, was at times formally applied to local dignitaries and to Imperial functionaries, in a manner which indicates that it was not felt to be excessive or invidious. I record in this section data earlier than Constantine's reign, and in the next section later material; others will no doubt be able to supply further instances.

About the beginning of our era C. Iulius Xenon of Thyatira died, and the citizens dedicated a Xenoneon to him as to a *heros euergetes* (which is more than was then done for governors) and the text recording this action speaks of his services to Asia and says of him, "having become in all things *soter* and *euergetes* and *ktistes* (founder) and *pater* of his fatherland." [38] This is strong language, for anything like *pater patriae* was hereafter in general used only of the Emperor. Now Xenon had been high priest of Augustus and Dea Roma—that is to say, an outspoken loyalist; so it is inconceivable that either Thyatira or the Iouliastai, the gild responsible for the maintenance of Xenon's cultus, would have thought that they were in any sense ascribing to Xenon—though the recipient of cult as a hero—a status which was too exalted for a commoner. (Augustus was probably still living).[39] Another

---

D. Magie, *op. cit.*, p. 1581, dates his governorship in 2/3 A.D. For contests in honor of Republican governors and for games at Alexandrea Troas, which were long called Smintheia Pauleia (associating the proconsul with the games as Kaisareia and Sebasta associated celebrations of games with the emperor), cf. H. Seyrig, *Rev. Arch.* 1929, i, p. 95, n. 4. Paulus fell within the Augustan period. The procurator Gemenus, who received *isotheoi timai* at Megalopolis (Insc. Gr. V, ii, 43–5) is assigned by Groag (col. 148 of work cited n. 58) to the first or second century. The restoration seems doubtful.

[38] J. Keil–A. v. Premerstein, *Denkschr. Wien* LIV, ii (1911), pp. 41 f.

[39] For the date cf. A.v. Premerstein, *Vom Werden u. Wesen d. Prinzipats* (*Abh. Bayer. Akad.* N.F. XV, 1937), p. 168. I do not discuss honors paid to Agrippa (cf. M. Reinhold, *Marcus Agrippa*, pp. 107, 133), since he came to occupy a position so close to what was from the Greek standpoint the monarchy. So did Sejanus; note that Tac. *Ann.* IV 2.4 speaks of Tiberius as *permitting* reverence to his images.

loyalist, Potamon, was honored on Mytilene as *euergetes* and *soter*
and *ktistes* of his fatherland. So in 10 A.D. the inhabitants of Lindos,
in dedicating to the gods a statue of the priestess of Athena, described her as *soter* and *euergetis*. (Be it observed that a contemporary text mentioning the statue does not repeat these epithets.)
Again, an inscription at Eumeneia in Phrygia describes a priest of
Roma as a *"soter* and *euergetes* as his ancestors were before him,"
and is likewise probably Augustan.[40] Prosecutors did indeed hold
it against a family that their ancestor Theophanes had received
divine honors (on Lesbos); [41] but this was under the suspicious
regime of Tiberius, and must be regarded as a piece of special
pleading. In any event, Nero, for all his amour propre, did not
object to the assumption by Milichus of the sobriquet Soter.

Somewhat later Gytheum honored Claudius Atticus, the father
of the famous Herodes, as *"kedemon* of the province and the city's
soter and *ktistes"*; [42] and a group of *mystai* at Tralles hailed an
agoranomos who was also *logistes* (i.e., *curator*) as *"soter* and
ktistes of his fatherland." [43] He had Imperial responsibilities but
was a local man.[44]

[40] For Potamon cf. Dittenberger, *Syll.* 754, *Inscr. gr.* XII *Supp.* 43 (and
for his loyalism, *I.G.R.R.* IV 60; *ib.* 95, his son as highpriest of Thea Roma
and Sebastos Zeus Caesar Olympios). For the Lindian evidence cf. Chr. Blin-
kenberg, *Lindos* II, cols. 747 ff., nos. 392 and 394; for the Eumeneia text,
I.G.R.R. IV 741.

[41] Tac. *Ann.* VI 18; West, *Corinth* VIII, ii, pp. 47 f. But no one minded the
image and temple set up by Prusa for the mother of Dio (Dio XLIV 2).

[42] *Inscr. gr.* V, i, 1171 (= II, ed. 2, 3596). If a fragmentary inscription at
Olympia (Dittenberger-Purgold, *Inschr. Ol.*, no. 622) is rightly restored, his
famous son appears there as *euergetes* and *soter*.

[43] Robert, *Rev. Phil.* LV (1929), pp. 138 ff. On these *mystai* cf. Ruge in
Pauly-Wissowa, VI A, col. 2123; religious groups often honored a public
character.

[44] A list of names on Thera (*Inscr. gr.* XII, iii, *Supp.* 1304) of Imperial
date includes what has been read as σωτὴρ στρατοῦ. No other name has anything by way of qualification and I am inclined to read as "Soter the son of
Stratos"; for Stratos as a proper name cf. Fr. Preisigke, *Namenbuch*, col. 396,
and Q. Smyrn. VIII 99.

On the other hand, we may note *Tituli Asiae minoris*, II, iii, 768, from
Arneae in Lycia, describing a man as having become *euergetes* and *soter* of

What has been recorded about Theophanes shows that tributes to local worthies could occasionally be noticed in the world at large; but much more was at stake when Imperial governors or *praefecti praetorio* were honored. To be sure, even that might be regarded as less significant when the honor was a momentary expression. From the time of Augustus onwards the governor of Egypt and lesser dignitaries were in petitions and other communications called *soter* and *euergetes*, etc.[45] This was the continuation of the style used to the king under the Ptolemaic regime;[46] then it had been almost confined to him,[47] but the change was logical, since, save where Roman citizens were concerned, the governor had the last word. So also a popular assembly, held at Oxyrhynchus about 300 A.D. to honor a *prytanis*, gave abundant acclamations not only to the Augusti but also to the *praeses* and the *katholikos* (both of whom were present) and to the *prytanis* him-

---

the People, is dated *paulo ante Christum*. Further, *Inscr. gr.* XII, iii, 519, on Thera, in which a Roman is honored by four men as their *soter* and *euergetes*, may well be contemporary. (Professor Dow informs me that the lettering used had its great vogue in Athens ca. 30–1 B.C.). Client kings were naturally described by the term *soter*; e.g., *I.G.R.R.* I, 879. It is likewise not surprising to find the dowager Empress Plotina referring to Epicurus as "the *soter*" (Dittenberger, *Syll.* 834.20), for she was writing to the Epicurean school at Athens as a professed devotee and employed Epicurean style. *Soter*, as applied to a doctor in Luc.(?) *Ocypus* 78, parodies tragic style.

[45] Even "of all men." Cf. Wilcken, *Arch. Pap.-Forsch.* VI (1913), p. 283; S. Eitrem, *P. Osloenses*, III, p. 189; *P. Mich.* 422.32, with the note of Youtie and Pearl. Cf. Philo, *Flacc.* 126, on the compliments formerly given by Isidorus and Lampon to Flaccus.

[46] H. Henne, *Bull. inst. fr. arch. orient.* XXI (1923), p. 204; cf. P. Collomp, *Rech. chancellerie des Lagides*, p. 96; *P. Enteuxeis*, 11.6 (ed. O. Guéraud); *P. Tebt.* 740 and 769.88; E. Bikerman, *Rev. hist. rel.* CXV (1937), p. 188.

[47] W. Schubart, *Arch. Pap.-Forsch.* XII (1936), p. 13; the exception which he notes (Dittenberger, *Or. gr. inscr. sel.* 194, on which cf. now A. Wilhelm, *Sitzungsber. Wien*, CCXXIV, i, 1946, pp. 24 ff.) is a formal decree by the priests of Amonrasonther in honor of the governor, giving him other exceptional distinctions—but this was in the troubled time of 42 B.C. The address to a lower official, Zeno, in *P. Cairo Zen.* 59482, also noted by S., involves a verbal statement and not an epithet, ὥσπερ οὖν διατελεῖς πάντας σῴζων (so also Aristeas 281. Cf. Wilcken, *Urk. Ptol.-Zeit*, nos. 52.8 f., "we have no helper save you and Sarapis," in an appeal to the *Hypodioiketes*).

self.[48] The *praeses* is addressed as *euergetes* and as "*soter* of decent people"; the *katholikos* is addressed as *euergetes* and receives the request, "Save the city for our Lords." The *prytanis* is called "author of blessings, *ktistes* of the city" and *kedemon* (protector). These frenzied compliments were indeed set down in writing, but are less important than formal votes recorded on stone.

The decree speaking of games in honor of Censorinus was mentioned earlier; it describes him as *soter* and *euergetes*. That he was a popular character is indicated by the phrase of Velleius Paterculus (II. 102.1), *virum demerendis hominibus genitum*: as a result of his administration of Pontus, Sinope called him "*kedemon* of the city," using a title essentially human and denoting a sympathetic interest.[49]

Later evidence is presented in tabular form on the following pages:

[48] Wilcken, *Chrest.* 45; Hunt-Edgar, *op. cit.*, p. 144, no. 239; cf. G. Méautis, *Hermoupolis-la-grande*, p. 198, and K. Latte, *Nachr. Göttingen*, 1945, p. 10. The prytanis asks for the honors to be deferred to a legitimate occasion, presumably at the end of his term of office; cf. the governor's objection to what seemed to him a premature tribute to Opramoas (*I.G.R.R.* III 739, vii; Magie, *op. cit.*, pp. 533 f. For a revised edition of the text cf. *Tit. Asiae min.* II, iii, 905).

[49] D. M. Robinson, *Am. J. Arch.* IX (1905), pp. 309 f., with useful quotation from Plat. *Rep.* 412C. E. Kornemann, *Neue Dokumente zum lakonischem Kaiserkult* (*Abh. schles. Ges. vaterl. Kultur*, I, 1929), p. 27, notes an instance in which it appears to be less dignified than *euergetes*; cf. v. Premerstein, *Werden*, p. 131, n. 2.

Official	Title	Giver	Details	Date
T. Iulius Celsus Polemaeanus, governor of Cappadocia, etc.	(their) *euergetes* and *soter*	City of Sardis	He probably came from Sardis	Under Titus [50]
C. Antius A. Iulius Quadratus, governor of Lycia, etc.	*soter* and *euergetes* of our city and of all within it, jointly and individually	Council and city of Lydae		Under Domitian [51]
Mettius Modestus, governor of Lycia, etc.	*soter* and *euergetes* of our city and of all within it, jointly and individually	Council and city of Lydae		ca. 100/2 [52]
Quadratus, as governor of Asia	*soter* and *euergetes* of the city	Council and city of Pergamum		ca. 108/9 [53]
T. Licinius Mucianus, governor of Galatia	*ho soter*	Unknown	In formula giving date	Second century [54]
Fulvius Titianus, *Legatus Augusti* and *curator*	[*soter*] and *euergetes* of the city	Council and people of Palmyra		First half of second century [55]
Claudius Iullus, *Legatus pro praetore*	*euergetes* and *soter* of the people	Council and people of Heraclea Salbace		End of second century [56]

		Citizen of Ephesus (probably)		170/1 [57]
[M. Nonius] Macrinus, governor of Asia	soter of the province			
Cn. Claudius Leonticus, governor and corrector of Achaea	soter of the [city]	Head of Delphic temple	He had repaired the temple and restored its lands	First quarter of third century [58]
P. Petronius Polianus, governor of Cappadocia	soter of the province	Italian colony at Nicopolis		Mid third century [59]
Unknown praefectus praetorio	soter and euergetes of the city	Termessus		Before end of third century [60]

[50] W. H. Buckler-D. M. Robinson, *Sardis*, VII, i, pp. 61 f., no. 45. (*Ib.*, p. 54, no. 33, we have another *soter* and *ktistes*. The editors suggest that it is a proconsul, but could it be Caligula?)

[51] *I.G.R.R.* III 520; cf. J. A. O. Larsen, *Class. Phil.* XXXVIII (1943), p. 189.

[52] *I.G.R.R.* III 523; Magie, p. 1599.

[53] *I.G.R.R.* IV 383; Magie, p. 1583.

[54] *Supp. epigr. gr.* VI 14.

[55] H. Seyrig, *Syria* XXII (1941), pp. 243 f. ("*soter*" and "our city" are most probable restorations).

[56] Buckler-Calder, *Monumenta Asiae minoris antiqua*, VI, 103; dated by Flacelière-Robert, *Rev. ét. gr.* LII (1939), p. 502.

[57] Dessau, *Inscr. lat. sel.* 8830; cf. A. Wilhelm, *Rhein. Mus.* LXXVII (1928), pp. 180 f., and P. Lambrechts in *Pauly-Wissowa*, XVII, cols. 879 ff. Wilhelm's restoration seems certain.

[58] Dittenberger, *Syll.* 877A; E. Groag, *Die römischen Reichsbeamten v. Achaia bis auf Diokletian* (*Schr. d. Balkankommission, Ant. Abt.* IX, 1939), col. 88.

[59] H. Grégoire, *Bull. Corr. Hell.* 1909, p. 35; cf. A. Stein, *Die Reichsbeamten v. Dazien* (*Dissertationes Pannonicae*, I, xii, 1944), p. 99.

[60] *Tit. Asiae minoris*, III, i, 126.

These data are scattered but not without significance. The terminology employed was clearly not exceptional: in particular, one instance seems clearly to fall under Domitian and to show that, in spite of his extreme emphasis on Imperial absolutism and its religious trappings, there was nothing in this which was in danger of savoring of lèse-majesté.[61]

III

We come now to four applications of *soter* and *euergetes* to high officials after the recognition of Christianity by Constantine.[62] About 330–4 the city of Sparta described the governor of Achaea as the "constant *euergetes* and *soter* of Sparta." [63] About 350 the Council of the city of Tralles set up an inscription in verse calling the proconsul of Asia *soter, ktistes*.[64] In more formal style, in the eighth decade of the century, the governor of Crete in accordance with a divine *thespisma* (i.e., an Imperial *constitutio*) and a decree of the province set up a statue of Petronius Probus, *praefectus praetorio* (now one of the highest officers of state); the

[61] Cf. the story about Theophanes' descendants (p. 139, earlier).

[62] Professor Dow has kindly communicated an additional instance which he is about to publish. He has deciphered *"euergetes* of Greece and *soter* of the Corinthians" in *Corinth* VIII, i, no. 108 (ed. B. D. Meritt), an inscription which has hitherto been regarded as completely erased except for the *ps(ephismati) b(oules)* at the bottom. The word "Corinthians" is not positive, but the other words quoted are clear and certain. The name of the man so honored is only partly legible, but definitely he was the provincial governor, and of sufficient consequence first to receive by vote of the Council a statue with such an inscription and subsequently to have his statue thrown down and the inscription erased. All the indications point to a date in the fourth century.

[63] A. M. Woodward, *Ann. Brit. Sch. Ath.* XXIX (1927/8), pp. 35 ff., L. Robert, *Hellenica*, IV, p. 21. (E. Groag, *Die Reichsbeamten v. Achaia in spätrömischer Zeit, Diss. Pannon.* I, xiv, pp. 25 f., puts the *terminus ante quem* in 333. He rightly remarks that the use of *soter* does not justify any inferences as to the governor's religious beliefs at the time of the honor.) For Spartan gratitude to another governor of this period cf. Woodward. *Ann.* XXVII (1925/6), pp. 245 ff.

[64] Robert, *l.c.*, pp. 112 f.

text speaks of Petronius as *euergetes* and *soter* of the province.[65]
Finally, about 397 the metropolis of Tralles (again "in accordance with divine decision") honored Flavius Caesarius, likewise a
praefectus praetorio; he was its *soter* and *euergetes* in all things.[66]
None of these texts is the utterance of a *Graeculus esuriens*, in-
different to official niceties; nor was this age of bureaucratic cen-
tralization likely to admit of divagations from the official line (as
municipalities under Tiberius had ignored his dislike of personal
worship).[67] The statements of Imperial approval no doubt refer
to the erection of a statue rather than to the wording of the inscription, but the wording had to be safe. We may infer that
soter and *euergetes* were politically neither provocative nor invidious. Can you imagine the unofficial application of *augustus* or
sebastos to a private individual? (The use of *sebastos* in a petition
to Herod the tetrarch in Malalas, p. 237.9, ed. Dindorf, must be
fictitious).

That is not all. These inscriptions were set up under Christian
Emperors. The first three fall within a period of tolerance, and
even in the time of the fourth the climate of opinion was somewhat more neutral than might be supposed.[68] Nevertheless, there
must have been limits to what would appear safe; Constantine
abolished the penalty of crucifixion because of its sacred associations.[69] Now *soter* was a title which belonged specially to Christ;

[65] M. Guarducci, *Riv. r. Ist. d'Arch.* I (1929), p. 171. In a text of 382/4
the Council of Olus in Crete honored their proconsul as *euergetes* (Robert,
pp. 103 ff.). I note this because of the context, though in general I have ab-
stained from citing instances of *euergetes* alone.

[66] Lebas-Waddington 1652d. On other honorific inscriptions of Tralles, and
on the frequency in them of *ktistes* cf. Ruge in *Pauly-Wissowa*, VI A, col. 2114.
On Caesarius, cf. J. R. Palanque, *La préfecture du prétoire du Bas-Empire*,
pp. 63, 86 ff., 92.

[67] Cf. Charlesworth, *Br. Sch. R.* XV, p. 3.

[68] Cf. G. Bardy, *L'église et les derniers Romains,* esp. ch. ii.

[69] Sozomen I 8 (*P.G.* LXVII, col. 881A) ; J. Vogt, *Festschrift Wenger*, II
(*Münch. Beitr. z. Papyrusforschung*, XXXV, 1944), p. 143.

in liturgical texts he is occasionally *soter* and *euergetes*.[70] As for Petronius, we must remember that he was baptized on his death-bed;[71] his family may well have shown Christian sympathies earlier and so he did himself, if a pseudo-Augustinian letter refers to him and is trustworthy.[72] Caesarius was presumably a professed Christian. All the same, *soter* so used was objectionable neither to these dignitaries nor to their masters.[73] *Soter* seems no longer to be used in inscriptions with reference to the emperor; but Julian says to Constantius that the good ruler is *soter* and *kedemon* to the city (p. 88B), while Themistius three times mentions *soter* among the epithets of divinity describing attributes which the emperor should imitate.[74] *Soter* was, therefore, still unexceptionable and still neu-tral in sense and capable of being used without any suggestion of other-worldly blessings. Further, common as was the idea that the functions of the king were parallel to those of God, and the sug-gestion that his moral qualities should show a similar correspond-

[70] H. Linssen, *Jahrb. f. Liturgiewissenschaft*, VIII (1928), p. 29.

[71] *Corp. inscr. lat.* VI 1756 (= *Carm. lat. epigr.* 1347). For his history in general cf. O. Seeck, *Symmachus*, p. CII and in *Pauly-Wissowa*, I, col. 2205; Palanque, *op. cit.*, pp. 109 ff. and in *Byzantion* IX, pp. 336 ff.

[72] *P.L.* XXXIII, col. 1175.

[73] On the political side, note three points. (1) *Cod. Iust.* I 24.1 records an enactment of 398 controlling the erection of statues to judges (to prevent such abuses as we know from the story of Verres, etc. Petronius Probus was suspected of engineering testimonials, cf. Amm. Marcell. XXX 5.8). (2) Seeck, *Gesch. d. Untergangs d. ant. Welt*, ed. 4, I, pp. 20, 444, suggests that Diocletian abandoned the habit of taking epithets commemorating victory in wars in which he or his partners had not personally taken part, because he did not wish to stress the success of subordinates. (3) Sensitiveness on the score of Imperial dignity is further suggested by what Asterius says about the re-moval of the purple from a soldier's garment, before it was burned when he had been found guilty of an offense and was given thus a vicarious punish-ment (E. Skard, *Symb. Oslo.* XXVII, 1949, pp. 58 ff., with references. Skard notes, *ib.*, XX, 1940, pp. 166 ff., that Asterius was interested in legal mat-ters).

[74] VI, p. 95.13, ed. Dindorf; IX, p. 151.5; XIX, p. 279.14 (references due to Professor Glanville Downey). For the emperor as *euergetes*, cf. K. M. Setton, *Christian Attitude Towards the Emperor in the Fourth Century*, p. 51.

ence, *soter* remained a word which was not too exalted for subordinates.

Thus Libanius remarks that magistrates expected to be called *soteres*,[75] and does this in a speech intended to influence Christian rulers. In spite of the added Christian association, *soter*, by itself or in association with *euergetes*, was as inoffensive as it had been to the monotheistic Josephus.[76] So in the second century a Bishop of Rome did not find Soter unsuitable for continued use as his personal name,[77] and later there is an instance of a Christian using Salvator in the same way.[78] Language is Protean and we must not force our logic upon it; Soter could describe a Messiah, but it

[75] XLV 20 (iii, p. 368.20, ed. Foerster) ; cf. R. A. Pack, *Studies in Libanius,* p. 113. Gothofredus, *Libanii . . . orationes quatuor, Notae,* p. 21, said well, "quae obseruatio jam passiua est." For an official as saving or having a hand in saving a city cf. Liban. XXI 19, 21, 25. (This speech is addressed to our Caesarius.) *Soteres* (*ib.* LXIV 78) describes great men of the past in retrospect; *soter* is used with deep feeling of Julian in XVIII 176 (cf. 232). In *Ep.* 803.5 a friend is called *soter* in the old manner of expressing gratitude. The ideal for an official is indicated in XXII 42; Hellebichus followed the Emperor as the Emperor followed God. For the feeling towards governors, cf. Himer. *Orat.* XIII 11, as also III 17, IV 9.

[76] So on occasion Philo (*Flacc.* 74; *Leg.* 22).

[77] Soter as a personal name had Jewish precedents (Diehl, *Inscr. chr. lat.* 4927. The same text includes Soteria as at woman's name). For a Christian having Sozon as a name cf. Diehl 3316.

[78] Diehl 3492D. Dean F. M. Rogers reminds me of the popularity later of Salvador and Salvatore as names. (So modern French usage does not wholly ban Dieu as a personal or place name, whatever its origin, e.g., "de Dieu.") I should not stress this point too much since the retention or giving of names derived from or identical with those of pagan deities was common among Christians. They cannot have been very sensitive on the point. (For the avoidance of a name on religious grounds cf. H. C. Youtie–C. Bonner, *Trans. Amer. Philol. Ass.* LXVIII, 1937, p. 49—on Eve; Foerster in Kittel, *Theol. Wörterb.* III. p. 286—on the disuse of Jesus as a Jewish proper name from the second century.)

Note also πενήτων σωτηρία in a Christian epitaph (Robert, *Rev ét. gr.* LXI, 1948, p. 168) and the special sense of σωτήρια for which Ducange *s.v.* gives references.—It is something quite different when we find St. Nicolaus described as "another *soter*," etc. (G. Anrich, *Hagios Nikolaos,* II, p. 497) ; this is language expressing by analogy a deep belief in the saint's effectual power to aid.

On the history of the word *salvator,* cf. Chr. Mohrmann, *Vigiliae Chris-*

could also denote not what Verres was but what he should and could have been, and men liked the sound of the word.

My warmest thanks are due also to Professors Campbell Bonner, H. J. Cadbury, Sterling Dow, Glanville Downey and M. L. W. Laistner and to Mr. Zeph Stewart for their generous aid.

---

tianae, IV (1950), pp. 201 ff. It was preferred to *servator, conservator* because the Christians (perhaps above all the Latin Christians) felt a need for precision which was not hampered by rhetorical and grammatical purism (on which cf. Nock, *Coniectanea Neotestamentica*, XI, pp. 163 ff.). Did Apuleius feel the need for a stronger and more colorful equivalent for *soter?* He uses *sospitator* seven times at least (D. S. Robertson on *Met.* IV 7, p. 12) and *sospitatrix* three times. *Sospitator* appears elsewhere in Arnobius and on the coins of Septimius Severus and his sons. Septimius came from the province of Africa and I venture to conjecture that this is an Apuleian coinage, based on the archaic sospitare (Enn. *Sc.* 295, p. 174, ed. Vahlen; Plaut. *Asin.* 683; Lucil. 739, ed. Marx). In view of Professor Chr. Mohrmann's suggestion that *sospitator* may be an old word, I do not press this.

NOTE: Since these pages went to press, Prof. M. Grant's important paper in *Num. Chron.* 1949, pp. 150 ff., has through the author's kindness reached me. Grant here discusses the portrayal of governors and others on local issues of coins in Asia Minor and Greece under the early empire. They even figure on the obverses. One man is on a reverse described as *euergetes*.

In this respect also what was done did not carry as much significance as we might have been tempted to think; but such portrayal on coins, unlike the use of the terms *soter* and *euergetes*, did not continue into the late empire.

Publications of Frederick Clifton Grant

St. Paul's Mysticism. *The Biblical World*, XLIV [Dec. 1914] 375–387.
A paper read to the Philosophy Club, General Theological Seminary, 1912.

St. Paul and Stoicism. *The Biblical World*, XLV [May 1915] 268–281.
Part of a B.D. thesis submitted to the Faculty of the General Theological Seminary; read to the Origen Society, 1912.

The Mission of the Disciples. Matt. 9:35–11:1 and Parallels. *Journal of Biblical Literature*, XXXV [1916] 293–314.

The Permanent Value of the Primitive Christian Eschatology. *The Biblical World*, XLIX [March 1917] 157–168.
Presidential Address to the Rock River Valley Ministerial Association, Dixon, Illinois, November 13, 1916.

The Eschatology of the Second Century. *The American Journal of Theology*, XXI [April 1917] 193–211.
Part of an S.T.M. Thesis submitted to the Faculty of the Western Theological Seminary, Chicago, 1916.

The Gospel of the Kingdom. *The Biblical World*, L [Sept. 1917] 129–191.
Five lectures to the Church School Teachers Association, St. Mark's Pro-Cathedral, Grand Rapids, 1912.

Peter Sat by the Fire. *The American Church Monthly*, IX [Aug. 1918].

A New Testament Bibliography, 1914–1917. *Anglican Theological Review*, I. 58–91.

Editorial Style in the Synoptic Gospels: I. St. Matthew. *Anglican Theological Review*, I. 278–287.

Editorial Style in the Synoptic Gospels: II. St. Luke. *Anglican Theological Review*, III. 51–58.

The Message of the Book of Jonah. *The American Church Monthly*, VI [Nov. 1919] 287–295.

A Critique of "Matthew's Sayings of Jesus" by George D. Castor. *Anglican Theological Review*, II. 27–34.

A Critique of "The Style and Literary Method of Luke" by Henry J. Cadbury. *Anglican Theological Review*, II. 318–323.

The Son of Barachiah. *Anglican Theological Review*, IV. 70–74.

The Life and Times of Jesus. The Abingdon Religious Education Texts (Week Day School Series, edited by George Herbert Betts). Abingdon Press, 1921. *Teacher's Manual*, 1922.

The Early Days of Christianity. The Abingdon Religious Education Texts, Abingdon Press (Week Day School Series), 1922. *Teacher's Manual*, 1926.

The Economic Significance of Messianism. *Anglican Theological Review*, VI. 196–213; VII. 281–289.

Part of a Dissertation submitted to Western Theological Seminary, Chicago, in partial fulfilment of the requirements for the degree of Th.D.

The Anglican Theological Review, VI–XXXIII. Edited since March 1924.

In addition to numerous articles, the editor has contributed many book reviews, signed and unsigned (including all unsigned notes on new books since 1918).

The Resurrection of Our Lord. In *Papers and Addresses at the Priests' Convention*, Philadelphia, April 29–30, 1924, edited by Selden Peabody Delany. *The American Church Monthly*, XV [June 1924] 273–287.

The Way of Peace. Three Devotional Addresses to Women. Milwaukee, Morehouse, 1924.

Quiet Day meditations for the Woman's Auxiliary of the Diocese of Chicago.

A New Testament Bibliography for 1918 to 1922 Inclusive. *Anglican Theological Review*, VI. 309–319; VII. 40–54.

The Modern Study of Plotinus. *Anglican Theological Review*, VII. 23–31.

The Place of Miracles in Religion. In *Problems of Faith and Worship*, edited by Charles L. Slattery. Macmillan, 1926. 120–145. Also published in the *Church Quarterly Review*, London.

A paper read at the St. Louis Church Congress in 1925.

The Place of the Bible in the Seminary Curriculum. *Report* of Fifth Biennial Meeting of the Conference of Theological Seminaries and Colleges in the United States and Canada, 1926, pp. 30–37.

The Life of St. Paul: Five chapters in *An Outline of Christianity*, Vol. I, *The Birth of Christianity:* edited by Ernest F. Scott and Burton Scott Easton. New York: Bethlehem Publishers (distributed by Dodd, Mead, and Co.), 1926. Also published in England by Waverley Book Co., London.

The Economic Background of the Gospels. Oxford: At the Clarendon Press, 1926.

The People and the Book. Abingdon Press, 1927.
A six-months course of lessons in Biblical Geography for church school teachers.

The Outlook for Theology. *Anglican Theological Review*, X. 1–10.
An address delivered at the Annual Commencement of Nashotah House, May 19, 1927, and at the Semicentennial of the Founding of the Divinity School of the University of the South, Sewanee, June 11, 1927.

An Outline of Theological Study. Evanston: Western Theological Seminary, 1928.

Method in Studying Jesus' Social Teaching. In *Studies in Early Christianity*, Presented to Frank Chamberlin Porter and Benjamin Wisner Bacon. Edited by S. J. Case. New York and London: Century, 1928, pp. 239–281.

Divorce: Another View. *Anglican Theological Review*, XI. 1–22.

New Horizons of the Christian Faith. Milwaukee: Morehouse; London: Mowbray, 1928.
The Hale Lectures for 1927–1928.

The Philosophic Study of Religion. *The Open Court*, XLIII [Jan. 1929] 16–31.
A lecture delivered at Northwestern University, Nov. 15, 1928.

The History of Christian Thought: A Reading Course. *Anglican Theological Review*, XII. 170–174.

To What Extent are the Articles of the Christian Faith as Contained in the Apostles' Creed Subject to Change or Revision? In *The Church and the Future* (record of the Church Congress for 1929), ed. by Chas. L. Slattery. New York: Gorham, 1929, pp. 82–99.

The Faith of the United Church. *Anglican Theological Review*, XII. 501–509.

Economic Messianism and the Teaching of Jesus. *Anglican Theological Review*, XII. 443–447.
>   Part of a Dissertation submitted to Western Theological Seminary, Chicago, for the degree of Th.D.

Adult Religious Education. *Anglican Theological Review*, XIII. 314–322.
>   An address to the Alumni of the Episcopal Theological School, Boston, Feb. 11, 1931.

The Beginnings of Our Religion: Outline of a Study Course. *Anglican Theological Review*, XIV. 314–339.

The Beginnings of Jesus' Ministry. *Journal of Biblical Literature*, LII. 189–202.

Mass or Holy Communion. *Anglican Theological Review*, XV. 27–38.

World Cooperation through Religion. In *World Fellowship*, a volume published by the First World Fellowship of Faiths. Chicago: Century of Progress Exposition, 1933.

The Growth of the Gospels. New York: Abingdon Press, 1933.
>   Lectures at the Summer School, University of Bishop's College, Lennoxville, Quebec, 1931.

All in the winter cold He came. *The Living Church*, Dec. 23, 1933 (cover).
>   A Christmas carol.

The Teaching of Jesus. In *The Institute*, XVIII. 63–68. University of Chicago: American Institute of Sacred Literature, 1934.

The Authority of the Church. *Anglican Theological Review*, XVI. 85–94.
>   A paper read to The Wrangler's Club, Chicago, Jan. 22, 1934.

Bishop Barnes's Gifford Lectures. *Anglican Theological Review*, XVI. 210–215.

Three chapters in *The Quest for God through Worship*. Ed. by Philip Henry Lotz, Bethany Press, 1934.
>   Ch. VI. The Quest for God through Creeds, pp. 40–43.
>   Ch. XXV. The Quest for God through Stewardship, pp. 116–119.
>   Ch. XXXVI. The Quest for God through Life-Partnership, pp. 160–163.

Sources of Our Faith and Our Faith in the Sources: II. The New Testament. In *Liberal Catholicism and the Modern World*, Vol. I, *Belief*, ed. by Frank Gavin. Milwaukee: Morehouse, 1934, pp. 43–53.

Form Criticism: A New Method of Research. *Religion in Life*, III. 351–366.

The Place of the Christian Tradition in Theological Education. *Report of the Ninth Biennial meeting of the Conference of Theological Seminaries and Colleges in the United States and Canada*, 1934, pp. 43–53.

Form Criticism: A New Method of New Testament Research. Chicago: Willett, Clark, 1934.
Including translations of Rudolf Bultmann's The Study of the Synoptic Gospels, and Karl Kundsin's Primitive Christianity in the Light of Gospel Research.

The Beginnings of Our Religion (edited). By F. James, C. B. Hedrick, B. S. Easton, and F. C. Grant. London: Society for Promoting Christian Knowledge; New York: Macmillan, 1934. Chapters by F. C. G.: V. Early Judaism; VI. Our Lord; X. The Evolution of Our Religion.

The Spiritual Christ. *Journal of Biblical Literature*, LIV [1935] 1–15. Presidential address to the Society of Biblical Literature and Exegesis, Dec. 27, 1934.

Further Thoughts on the M-Hypothesis. Edinburgh: *Expository Times*, XLVI [1935] 438–445.

Letter to a Friend Entering a Seminary. In *The Churchman*, Oct. 15, 1935, pp. 16, 33, 35.

Why the Church? London: *The Congregational Quarterly*, XIII [Jan. 1935] 11–22.

Record of a Conference Between the Committee of Comity of the Evangelical Lutheran Augustana Synod and the Sub-Committee of the Joint Commission for Conference on Church Unity of the Protestant Episcopal Church. Held at Seabury-Western Theological Seminary, Evanston, Illinois, Dec. 3–4, 1935 (edited; pp. 44).

Some Ideals of Education in Religion. *Religion in Life*, IV. 364–375.

Worship and Experience. *Anglican Theological Review*, XVII. 65–82. Reprinted in *Religious Digest*, I. 6–8.

Frontiers of Christian Thinking. Chicago: Willett, Clark, 1935. Lectures to the Chicago Congregational Union, at the Tower Hill Convocation, held at Sawyer, Michigan, Sept. 1934.

Two New Testament articles in *A New Standard Bible Dictionary*, 3rd ed. [Gospels, and Synoptic Problem]. New York: Funk and Wagnalls, 1936.

Seabury-Western Theological Seminary. *Historical Magazine of the Protestant Episcopal Church*, V. 306–311.

The Future of Protestantism, *Christendom*, I. 240–252.

Faith by Works. *The Christian Century*, Feb. 5, 1936.
> A sonnet in memory of George Herbert Thomas, Rector of St. Paul's Church, Chicago.

The Upward Look. Two meditations and prayers (June 9, Nov. 3) in a volume of daily devotions, edited by Harold Garnet Black and Gaius Glenn Atkins. Houghton, Mifflin, 1936.

Horace, Ode V. Quis multa gracilis. *Chicago Tribune*, March 9, 1936.
> A translation of Odes I. 5.

Further Thoughts on Form Criticism. *Religion in Life*, V. 532–543.
> A paper read to the Mid-western Branch of the American Oriental Society, March 27, 1936.

The Function of the Church in the Modern World. *Journal of Religion*, XVI. 127–141.
> An address to the Faculties Union, Chicago, Nov. 1935.

The Ballad of Young Isaac. *The Churchman*, CL. 15 (Christmas, 1936).
> A Christmas ballad.

The History of Primitive Christianity. By Johannes Weiss. Completed by Rudolf Knopf after the author's death. Translated by Four Friends and edited by F. C. G. Two volumes. New York: Wilson-Erickson; London: Macmillan, 1936.
> Bk. I. The Primitive Community, tr. by F. C. G.
> Bk. II. The Gentile Mission and Paul the Missionary, tr. by Arthur Haire Forster.
> Bk. III. Paul the Christian and Theologian, tr. by Paul Stevens Kramer.
> Bk. IV. The Missionary Congregations and the Beginnings of the Church; and Bk. V. The Separate Areas, tr. by Sherman Elbridge Johnson.

The Gospel and the Canon Law [on Marriage]. *The Churchman*, Sept. 1, 1937 (4 pp.).

Invocation. *Harvard Divinity School Bulletin*, XXXIV, no. 16, p. 4.
> A hymn addressed to the Holy Spirit; it was read at a Chapel Service of the Harvard Divinity School during the observance of the Tercentenary of Harvard University in 1936.

The Episcopal Church: Its Contribution to the Religious Life of America. *Anglican Theological Review*, XIX. 1–16.
> A paper read at the Tercentenary of the Harvard Divinity School, June 25, 1936, as one of a number representing the various religious traditions in America.

Spiritualizing the Secular. A paper read at the 17th Annual Episcopal Social Work Conference, Indianapolis, 1937; printed in *Episcopal Social Work*, 1937, pp. 13–19.

The Permanence of Christianity. *Anglican Theological Review*, XIX. 112–118.

Part One of the Church Congress Syllabus Number I, on The Basis of Christian Faith and Action Today.

Form Criticism Farther Afield. *Anglican Theological Review*, XIX. 181–186.

A critique of "The Growth of Literature" by H. M. and N. K. Chadwick, Vols. I–II, Cambridge University Press, 1932, 1936.

Was the Author of John Dependent upon the Gospel of Luke? *Journal of Biblical Literature*, LVI. 285–307.

Presenting Religion to Youth. *Religion in Life*, VI. 381–391.

The Quest for God through Understanding. Ed. by Philip Henry Lotz. Bethany Press, 1937.

Ch. VII. The Quest for God through World Brotherhood, pp. 40–46.

Ch. VIII. The Quest for God through Repentance, pp. 47–54.

The Choirmaster and the Clergyman. No. 10 in *The Church and Choral Music Series*. Northwestern University Information, Nov. 4, 1937.

A lecture at Northwestern University School of Music.

The Communion of Saints as Interpreted by the Anglican Church. *Report* No. 2 of the Commission of the Church's Unity in Life and Worship for the World Conference on Faith and Order, Edinburgh, 1937, ed. by Gaius Jackson Slosser. New York: Harper, 1937, pp. 33–37.

Christianity and War. A Witness tract, 1938.

The Birthday Prayer of a Platonist. In *Muse: An Anthology of Current Poetry*. New York: Carlyle Straub, 1938.

A sonnet.

Evangelical Spirit and Tradition in the Theological Seminaries. In *Abiding Values of Evangelicalism:* Papers and Addresses at the 75th anniversary of the Evangelical Education Society of the Protestant Episcopal Church, Feb. 8–9, 1938, pp. 115–134.

The Basic Formula for Church Union (Chs. I and II). Edited by Douglas Horton. Chicago Theological Seminary and Seabury Western Theological Seminary, 1938.

156 *A List of the Publications of Frederick Clifton Grant*

God and His World: Bible Readings and Meditations for the Summer, 1938 (June 13–Aug. 6). Published in *Forward Day by Day*, Forward Movement Commission, Cincinnati.

Studies in the Text of St. Mark. *Anglican Theological Review*, XX. 103–119.

Faith and Knowledge. Inaugural Address at Union Theological Seminary. *Alumni Bulletin*, Nov. 1938.

Foreword to *Seventy Stories of the Old Testament*, illustrated with reproductions from work of master woodcut artists of the 15th and 16th centuries. Compiled by Helen Slocum Estabrook. Portland, Me.: The Bradford Press, 1938. Also Foreword to the New Testament volume, published in 1945.

Why Change the Bible? *Religion in Life*, VII. 510–524.

The Nature of the Church: Part I. Historical Origins. *Anglican Theological Review*, XXI. 190–204. Church Congress Syllabus, IV. 1.

Did the Jews Crucify Jesus? *The Christian Century*, LVI [Mar. 1, 1939] 275–276.

Form Criticism and the Christian Faith. *Journal of Bible and Religion*, VII [Feb. 1939] 9–17 and 48.

A Note on Dr. Peritz's Article [= an article by Dr. Ismar J. Peritz, pub. in the same number, "Form Criticism as I see it," in A Symposium on Form Criticism by Dr. Peritz, F. C. G., and Professor Mary E. Andrews]. *Ib.*, VII [Nov. 1939] 177–180.

The Church's Present Task. *Religion in Life*, VIII. 339–349.

The Significance of Divergence and Growth in the New Testament. *Christendom*, IV. 575–587.

The Proposed Concordat in the Light of the New Testament. *The Churchman*, January 1, 1939 (2 pp.).

A Personal Confession of Faith. In a volume edited by Philip Henry Lotz, Bethany Press, 1939.

The Message of Jesus Christ. By Martin Dibelius. (Translated.) New York: Scribner, 1939.

The Gospel and the Predicament of Modern Man (edited). The Washington Church Congress Papers, 1939. New York: The Church Congress, 1939.

Papers read at the Church Congress held at the Cathedral in Washington, D. C.

The Gospel in the New Testament. In *The Gospel and the Predica-*

ment of Modern Man: The Washington Church Congress Papers, 1939, pp. 10–24.

The Gospel of the Kingdom. New York: Macmillan, 1940.
The Haskell Lectures for 1940, delivered at the Oberlin Graduate School of Theology.

The Proposed Marriage Canon. *Anglican Theological Review*, XXII. 169–181.

The Significance of Critical Study of the Gospels for Religious Thought Today. In *Theology and Modern Life:* Essays in Honor of Harris Franklin Rall, edited by Paul A. Schilpp. Chicago: Willett, Clark, 1940, pp. 56–78.

The Proposed Concordat Between the Protestant Episcopal Church and the Presbyterian Church. *The Chronicle*, March 1940.
Also reprinted as a tract.

Syllabus on Approaches to Unity between the Presbyterian Church in the United States of America and the Protestant Episcopal Church in the United States of America (edited; pp. 40), 1940.

Form Criticism Still Farther Afield. *Anglican Theological Review*, XXII, 213–218.
A critique of "The Growth of Literature" by H. M. and N. K. Chadwick, Vol. III, Cambridge University Press, 1940.

Where Form Criticism and Textual Criticism Overlap. *Journal of Biblical Literature*, LIX. 11–21.

The Anglican Doctrine of the Sacraments. *Anglican Theological Review*, XXIII. 23–46.
One of the "Princeton Papers" on the Church, the Ministry, and the Sacraments, by Theodore O. Wedel, Angus Dun, and Frederick C. Grant, read at the joint meeting of the Commission on Approaches to Unity of the Protestant Episcopal Church and the Department of Church Cooperation and Union of the Presbyterian Church in the U.S.A., held at Princeton, New Jersey, June 18, 1940.

Realized Eschatology. *Christendom*, VI. 82–95.
A study of the views of Professor C. H. Dodd.

Eschatology and Reunion. *Religion in Life*, X. 83–91.

The Christ of the Gospels. *Religion in Life*, X. 430–441.

The Witness. Chairman of the Editorial Board 1941–45; Book Editor since 1945. Contributions: articles, editorials, book reviews, and notes on new books.

What We Believe. The Church Congress Study Book for 1942.

The Sermon on the Mount. *Anglican Theological Review*, XXIV. 131–144.

A critical review of "The Sermon on the Mount" by Martin Dibelius.

Was There a Document "Q"? *Religion in Life*, XI. 35–44.

Ethics and Eschatology in the Teaching of Jesus. *Journal of Religion*, XXII. 359–370.

An essay in the number of the *Journal of Religion* devoted to the memory of Shailer Mathews.

The Gospels and Civilization. *Religion in Life*, XII. 231–237.

The Conference on Theological Education called by the Presiding Bishop; Princeton, New Jersey, April 14–15, 1942. *Anglican Theological Review*, XXIV. 181–183.

Edward Gibbon's Five Causes. *Religion in Life*, XIII. 18–25.

The Earliest Gospel: Studies of the evangelic tradition at its point of crystallization in writing. Abingdon-Cokesbury, 1943.

The Cole Lectures for 1943, Vanderbilt University.

The Hymnal 1940. New York: The Church Pension Fund, 1943.

Professor Grant has been a member of the Church Hymnal Commission from its beginning, and served as a member of the Translations Committee and also as Chairman of the Committee on Carols.

Foreword to *Victorious Mountaineer:* A Memoir of Harry Peirce Nichols. By Wm. Bertrand Stevens. The Cloister Press, 1944.

In Memory of James Moffatt. *The Union Review*, VI [Dec. 1944] 3–4.

Can We Still Believe in Immortality? The Cloister Press, 1944.

Introducing the Gospel Story. Youth Division of the National Council of the Protestant Episcopal Church, 1945.

A Personal Confession of Faith. In *The Quest for God through Faith*, ed. by Philip H. Lotz, Wyoming, Illinois, 1944, pp. 60 f. Chicago, 1944.

The Idea of a Theological College. Kenyon College Bulletin, June, 1944.

A paper read at the Conference on Theological Education at Bexley Hall, 1944.

One Hundred Books for a Clerical Library. A list drawn up for the *Church Congress*, revised by the Rt. Rev. Henry St. George Tucker, D.D., Presiding Bishop of the Protestant Episcopal Church, and published by the Church Congress, 1944.

Christology and Gospel Research. *The New Christianity*, XI. 59–64.

Jesus Christ. In *Encyclopedia of Religion*, edited by Vergilius Ferm. New York: Philosophical Library, 1945.

Also articles on Gospel and the Gospels; Synoptic Gospels; Form Criticism, or Formgeschichte; etc.

Early Christian Baptism. *Anglican Theological Review*, XXVII. 253–263.

A paper read at the Episcopal Evangelical Conference in Wilmington, Delaware, in 1945.

Archbishop Temple and the Future. *The Union Review*, VII [Feb. 1945].

Revised Standard Version of the New Testament. New York: Thomas Nelson and Sons, 1946.

Professor Grant is one of the nine members of the New Testament committee which produced this revision of the American Standard edition of the Revised Version.

The Greek Text of the New Testament. Ch. V in *An Introduction to the Revised Standard Version of the New Testament*. International Council of Religious Education, 1946, pp. 37–43.

Apocalypse Up-to-Date. Columbia Broadcasting System *Talks*, April, 1946.

Quoted from a broadcast discussion of the Book of Revelation, on the "Invitation to Learning" program, Jan. 6, 1946—a triologue by T. V. Smith, George Shuster, and F. C. Grant.

The Practice of Religion. New York: Macmillan, 1946.

The Voice of the Cathedral. London: *The Christian World Pulpit*, CXLIX [Apr. 25, 1946] 132–134.

A sermon preached in the Cathedral of St. John the Divine, New York.

Preaching the Easter Message. *Anglican Theological Review*, XXVIII. 53–59.

Part I of a series, Preaching the Christian Year.

The Discipline of the Liberal. *The Witness*, XXIX. 46, pp. 8–10; 47, pp. 8–11 (Oct. 17, 24, 1946).

An address to the Younger Clergy of the Diocese of New York.

The Mind of Christ on Marriage. Ch. III in *Five Essays on Marriage*, by Burton Scott Easton, Frederick A. Pottle, Frederick C. Grant, W. Norman Pittenger, Sherman E. Johnson. Written at the request of the Joint Commission on Holy Matrimony; published by the Cloister Press at the request of the Episcopal Evangelical Fellowship, 1946, pp. 33–42.

Religion and Poetry. Ch. X in *Munera Studiosa* [Essays presented to William Henry Paine Hatch on his Seventieth Birthday], edited by Massey Hamilton Shepherd, Jr., and Sherman Elbridge Johnson. Cambridge, Episcopal Theological School, 1946, pp. 161–178. The paper was originally read to the Faculty Club, General Theological Seminary, April 19, 1945.

The Teaching of Jesus and First-Century Jewish Ethics, in *The Study of the Bible Today and Tomorrow*, by Members and Guests of the Chicago Society for Biblical Research, edited by Harold R. Willoughby. Chicago: The University of Chicago Press, 1946, pp. 298–313.

Protestant Episcopal Church. Article in the new edition of *Chambers's Encyclopaedia*. London, 1947.

Foreword to *Old Testament Stories in Woodcut*, by Helen Slocum Estabrook. Boston, Beacon Press, 1947.

Foreword to *Scenes from the Life of Jesus in Woodcut*, by Susan Nichols Pulsifer. *Ib.* (= reissue).

A New Greek-Latin New Testament. *Anglican Theological Review*, XXIX. 247–250.

A critique of Novi Testamenti Biblia Graeca et Latina, edited by Joseph M. Bover, S.J., Madrid, 1943.

Current New Testament Books. *Union Seminary Quarterly Review*, III [Jan. 1948] 23–27 [May 1949] 27–32.

New Testament and Church History articles in *The American College Dictionary*. New York: Random House, 1947.

Chiefly the review or revision of articles already prepared.

New Testament articles in the new edition of the *Encyclopaedia Britannica* (Gospels; Mark; Gospel of Mark). Chicago, 1948.

Revision of articles in the preceding edition.

Bible and Church History articles in the new edition of *World Book Encyclopedia* (for children). Chicago: World Book Encyclopedia, 1948.

Chiefly articles on Biblical and Church History subjects; some articles were revised, others were rewritten.

Nilsson's History of Greek Religion. *Anglican Theological Review*, XXX. 64–67.

A critique of Martin P. Nilsson, "Geschichte der Griechischen Religion," Bd. I: "Bis zur Griechischen Weltherrschaft," Munich, 1941.

The Church's One Foundation. *The Southern Churchman*, CXIV [Jan. 10, 1948] 5–7.

Educating for the Ministry. *Christendom*, XIII [1948] 360–372.

Lambeth and Unity. *The Churchman*, CLXII, pp. 7–8.

I Believe in God. *Religion in Life*, XVIII. 3–10.

The Goal of Christian Education. Convocation Sermon, University of Bishop's College, Lennoxville, Quebec, June 17, 1948. Published by the University.

Foreword to *Parson's Sampler* by J. W. Kennedy. New York: Morehouse-Gorham, 1948.

A New Book on the Parables. *Anglican Theological Review*, XXX. 118–121.

A critique of Joachim Jeremias, "Die Gleichnisse Jesu," Zürich, 1947.

Preaching the Christian Year: II. The Christmas Message. *Anglican Theological Review*, XXX. 227–230.

Christianity and Communism. *The Southern Churchman*, CXV. 15 (Apr. 9, 1949), pp. 3–5 and 9.

A sermon preached in St. Paul's Chapel, Columbia University.

Jesus. By Martin Dibelius. Translated by Charles B. Hedrick and Frederick C. Grant. Westminster Press, 1949.

The Divinity of Christ. *Religion in Life*, XVIII. 483–492.

The Social Teaching of the Prayer Book. *The Southern Churchman*, CXV [Feb. 5, 1949] pp. 3–5. Also published in *The Maryland Churchman*.

The address at the opening of the Convention of the Diocese of Maryland, Baltimore, Jan. 25, 1949, on the 400th anniversary of the Book of Common Prayer.

The World's Great Poetry. *Crozer Quarterly*, XXVI. 317–324.

Isaac Watts. *The Southern Churchman*, CXV [May 14, 1949] 4–5.

The Hymnal 1940 Companion. New York: Church Pension Fund, 1949.

F. C. G. contributed the first draft of the biographical sketches of about twenty minor hymn writers and composers.

Preaching the Christian Year: III. Palm Sunday. *Anglican Theological Review*, XXXII. 33–39.

The Citation of Greek Manuscript Evidence in an Apparatus Criticus. In *New Testament Manuscript Studies:* the Materials and the Making of a Critical Apparatus, a volume presented to Professor

Edgar J. Goodspeed, edited by Merrill M. Parvis and Allen P. Wikgren. Chicago: University of Chicago Press, 1950, pp. 81–94.

The Impracticability of the Gospel Ethics. In *Aux sources de la tradition chrétienne. Mélanges offerts à M. Maurice Goguel à l'occasion de son soixante-dixième anniversaire.* (Bibliothèque théologique.) Paris and Neuchatel: Delachaux et Niestlé, 1950, pp. 86–94.

Notes on Translating the New Testament. In *The Bible Translator*, edited by E. A. Nida, I. 145–149.

Protestant Law. In *Divorce and Domestic Relations*, a compilation of the Virginia Law Weekly *Dicta*, Vol. II, Charlottesville, 1949–50, pp. 10–13.

In Memoriam Burton Scott Easton. 1877–1950. *Anglican Theological Review*, XXXII. 89–91. Also published in the *Bulletin* of the General Theological Seminary, XXXVI. 5–8.

An Introduction to New Testament Thought. Abingdon-Cokesbury Press, 1950.

Preaching Values in the New Translations of the New Testament. *Bulletin* of the General Theological Seminary, XXXVI. 30–37. The Alumni Essay read at Commencement, May 24, 1950.

Exegesis, Biblical. Article in the new edition of *Encyclopedia Americana*, Vol. X. 628–636. New York, 1950. The article deals with the history of exegesis.

Illuminati. Article in the new edition of *Encyclopedia Americana*, 1950.

Christ's Victory and Ours: A Book for Good Friday and Easter. Macmillan, 1950.

Biblical Backgrounds. In *The Adult Teacher.* Lessons for August 1950–June 1951. Abingdon-Cokesbury Press. Introductions to the books of the New Testament.

Preaching Values in the Revised Standard Version. *Religion in Life*, XX. 114–132.

The Church Exists for the Sake of Its Mission. *The Southern Churchman*, CXVI (February 11, 1950) 3–4. A sermon preached in the Cathedral of St. John the Divine, New York.

Preaching the Christian Year: IV. Trinity Sunday. *Anglican Theological Review*, XXXIII. 18–23.

Self Consecration. *Union Seminary Quarterly Review*, VI. 5–6, 9. A chapel address, reprinted in *The Witness*.

Introduction and Commentary on Mark. In *The Interpreter's Bible*,
Vol. I. Abingdon-Cokesbury Press, 1951.
Fresh Light on Manicheism. *Anglican Theological Review*, XXXIII.
Hellenistic Religions: The Age of Syncretism. New York: Liberal
Arts Press, 1951.
Memorial volume to Burton Scott Easton. (Edited) 1951.

The above list does not include numerous book reviews in *The American
Church Monthly, American Historical Review, American Journal of Theol-
ogy, Anglican Theological Review, Christendom, The Christian Century,
The Churchman, Classical Philology, The Crozer Quarterly, Journal of Bible
and Religion, Journal of Biblical Literature, Journal of Religion, The Living
Church, The Pastor, Religion in Life, The Review of Religion, The Union
Seminary Quarterly Review, The Witness.*